SOLEMN
SILENCE

SOLEMN SILENCE

The complete guide to ...

**HOOD CANAL,
BY LAND,
AND SEA**

Wm. H. Schweizer

*Illustrations by
Richard Amundsen*

eos *publishing*

To Sherry, Johnny, Susie, Kristjan

EOS Publishing, 331 Andover Park East,
    Seattle, Washington 98188

Published 1992

Illustrations and design by Richard Amundsen
Photographs by William H. Schweizer unless otherwise
noted

Cover: Olympic Mountains, Hood Canal, United States,
summer, 1991.

Library of Congress Catalog Card Number 91-092471

ISBN 0-925244-02-3

Frontispiece: Twanoh State Park--Marine State Park,
Hood Canal, United States, summer, 1991.

Acknowledgments

I would like to thank the following individuals and organizations for their help and inspiration with this book: Jim Harris; Ron Baird, Eastman Kodak; Clyde McDonald; University of Puget Sound; Quilcene Pre-School Parent-Teachers Assn.; Pioneer Ladies Aid of Brinnon Community Church; Sally Huntingford; Irene Hodgdon; Sharon Tucker, The Washington State Governor's Office; Bob Caughie; Rick Caughie; Sandra L. Gourdin, Maurie Sprague, United States Department of the Interior; Jim DeShazo, John R. Freeman, Bill Freymond, Rocky Beach, Greg Schirato, Judy Hildebrandt, Susan Ewing, State of Washington Department of Wildlife; John McGlenn, Jim Walton, Washington State Wildlife Commissioners; Carlyle Staab, Randy Person, James L. Ellis, State Parks and Recreation Commission; Ann Morgan, Nick Handy, Theresa Rush, Dan Scamporlina, Margie Reed, Dan Barth, Tim Gregg, Jim Thomas, Lowell McQuoid, Doug Magoon, Mike Cronin, Reid Schuller, Blanche Sobottke, Washington State Department of Natural Resources; and Brian J. Boyle-Commissioner of Public Lands; Kenneth A. Gouldthorpe, State of Washington Department of Trade and Economic Development; Joanne Conrad, Tom Quinn, United States Department of Agriculture; Elaine Miller, Richard Frederick, Dr. James B. Rhoads, Marie DeLong, David Nicandri, The Washington State Historical Society; Brad O'Connor, The Seattle Times; Senator Peter von Reichebauer; Phyllis Gilven, Tacoma Public Utilities; Harold R. Garrett, Willis Whitney, O. R. (Bob) George, Washington State Department of Transportation; Dean Lollar, Chief Seattle Council, Boy Scouts of America; Ernie Gann; Jim Buckles; Bruce O. Bleckert, Custom Photo Service; Richard Amundsen; and John, Susan, Kristjan and Sherry Schweizer, my crew.

I am also thankful to the following individuals and organizations for their permission to use copyrighted material:

Drucker, Philip. From *Cultures of the North Pacific Coast,* by permission of Harper and Row, Publishers, Inc.

Lastly I would to thank you the reader who I invite to submit ideas, questions, and suggestions.

Contents

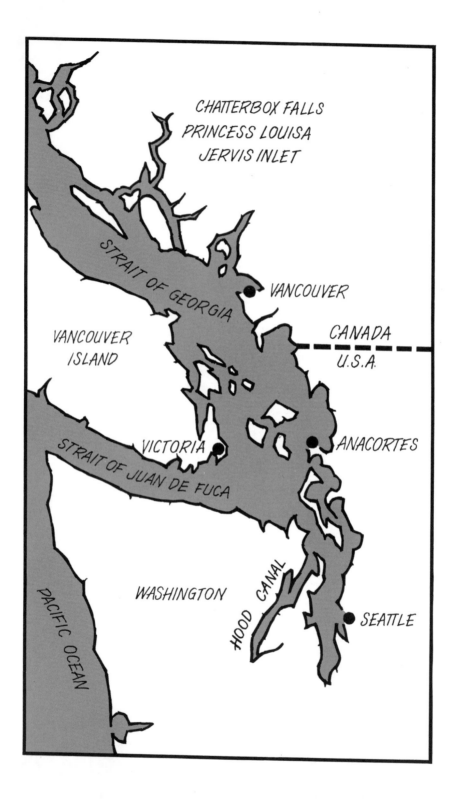

Chapter 1

HOOD CANAL

Hood Canal skirts the eastern edge of the Olympic Peninsula and from the peaks or higher levels of several mountains in the immediate vicinity of Quilcene a real Olympian view is presented to anyone who will take the time and make the effort to reach the higher levels. The view is Olympian in all senses--befitting or characteristic of Olympus or the Olympian Gods, as in power or dignity; godlike, awe-inspiring. Hence the name Olympic! A year around favorite retreat for those on vacation is beautiful 70-mile-long Hood Canal. From any location the visitor can enjoy salt water fishing, particularly salmon fishing in protected waters; fresh water, stream and lake fishing and salt water swimming, sailing or motoring. A broad highway encircles the entire Peninsula. You can leave any given point on Hood Canal and return to it by making the "Loop" trip.

The above quote was written over forty years ago in a Hood Canal cookbook. Not much has changed in this quote but obviously Hood Canal does see more people-- both tourists and residents. Fortunately, the essential character of Hood Canal is still the same as when Captain Vancouver experienced its "solemn silence" or in his own words, "the solemn silence that prevailed." *Solemn Silence: The Complete Guide to Hood Canal by Land and Sea*, is meant to be your guide to a very unique area of our land--traveler basics, past to present, native heritage, common plants, wildlife, sights along the way, exploring Hood Canal, Hood Canal kitchen home recipes, and memories of early pioneers. Like Captain Vancouver, I hope you will find your share of "solemn silence" on Hood Canal by land or sea, especially in our fast paced world. The following pictures give a glimpse of the "solemn silence" that can still be found on Hood Canal.

Little Mission Creek, Belfair State Park

Annas Bay, Hood Canal

Melbourne Lake

Mt. Ellinor

Olympic Mountains from Tahuya Peninsula

Olympic Mountains from Scenic Beach State Park

Hamma Hamma River

Lena Creek Campground, Olympic National Forest

Hood Canal from Webb Lookout Road

Hood Canal from Seamount

Falls View Canyon Trail, Falls View Campground

Mt. Walker

Hood Canal from Hood Canal Floating Bridge

Twin Lakes, Tahuya Peninsula

Chapter 2

TRAVELER BASICS

The goal of this chapter is to ensure you have a memorable and safe exploration of Hood Canal by land or sea.

PLANNING AND PREPARATION

The success of any exploration is directly related to the amount of time spent on planning and preparation. The more time spent on planning and preparation the more enjoyable your adventure will be.

MAPS AND CHARTS

For exploring Hood Canal by land I recommend the topographic maps contained in the *Washington Atlas & Gazetteer* by DeLorme Mapping Company.

For exploring Hood Canal by sea I recommend U.S. Chart 18476--Puget Sound, Hood Canal to Dabob Bay.

I also recommend: *Tide Tables, West Coast of North and South America; Tidal Current Tables, Pacific Coast of North America and Asia; United States Coast Pilot 7, Pacific Coast: California, Oregon, Washington, and Hawaii.* The *Coast Pilot* is an invaluable source of

information and explains general navigation in-
formation:routes, navigational hazards, vessel traffic
management, navigational information, buoyage, Coast
Guard, search and rescue and regulations, etc.; general
geographic information: communications, repair facilities,
etc.; natural conditions: tide, current information, sea
and swell, and climate information, etc. The *Coast Pilot*
also explains pertinent information regarding the chart
listed above: geographic descriptions, tides, beacons,
anchorage, weather, dangers, i.e. rocks, etc.

ROUTES TO HOOD CANAL

Hood Canal is easily accessible from anywhere in the
country. Coming from the east you would take I-90 to
Seattle, and coming from the north or south you would
take I-5 or U.S. Highway 101 to Seattle or Tacoma.
Hood Canal is also easily accessible from anywhere in
the world by flying to the Seattle-Tacoma International
Airport and then driving north on I-5 to Seattle or
south on I-5 to Tacoma. From Seattle take the Seattle-
Bremerton ferry to State Route 304 to State Route 3
south to Belfair. From Tacoma take I-5 south to State
Route 16 west, crossing the Tacoma Narrows Bridge, to
State Route 3 south to Belfair. Belfair is the gateway
to Hood Canal.

Seattle skyline and the Bremerton ferry

The Tacoma Narrows Bridge

Boeing 747 landing at Sea-Tac International Airport

WHEN TO GO

The Hood Canal area can be enjoyed all year.

LOW SANDSPITS AND FLATS

The symbols for sandspits and flats on your chart should be given the highest attention and respect. You should always know where you are on your chart and where any sandspits and flats are in relation to your boat no matter how beautiful and peaceful the day or how far you are from shore. You should always study and plot your course for the next day one day in advance and special attention should be given to the symbols for sandspits and flats. The *United States Coast Pilot 7* says:

> The dangers are few and generally close inshore. A few low sandspits from 100 to 300 yards long are difficult to see at night, but most of them have been made into resorts and the buildings nearby show up well against the background of trees. Flats off the mouths of streams extend as much as 0.5 mile offshore and are extensive at the heads of some of the bays. A midchannel course is clear until reaching The Great Bend, where Hood Canal turns E. Here the N shore just E of Ayres Point should be favored to clear the flats extending from the E part of Annas Bay.

FLOAT PLAN

Before departing on a cruise you should advise a responsible friend or relative where you will be going, when you will check in with him/her regarding your various destinations and when you will be back. Your friend or relative will need a detailed description of your boat. Tell this person if he/she doesn't hear from you by a certain date and time to notify the U.S. Coast Guard to start looking for you.

An excellent means of accomplishing the above is through "Float Plan" forms available through marine insurance companies or government agencies concerned with boating safety.

WATER

To prevent giardiasis, a debilitating intestinal disorder caused by drinking stream or lake water, rapidly boil for one full minute, chemically treat, or bring your own.

PSP

Before eating any shellfish, make sure the area is free of parallytic shellfish poisoning by calling the Washington State Department of Health's Red Tide Hotline at 1-800-562-5632. PSP is caused by a toxin produced by a small organism. This organism is eaten by the shellfish and stored in its body and is highly poisonous to human beings.

FISHING LICENSE

Regarding fishing license requirements please obtain *Washington Department of Wildlife, (current year), Game Fish Regulations, pamphlet edition.*

HUNTING LICENSE

Regarding hunting permit requirements please obtain *Washington Department of Wildlife, (current year), Hunting Seasons and Rules, pamphlet edition.*

SALMON, SHELLFISH, BOTTOMFISH LICENSE

Regarding salmon, shellfish, and bottomfish license requirements please obtain, *(current year), Salmon, Shellfish, Bottomfish, Sport Fishing Guide, Washington State Department of Fisheries.*

FIRE

Adhering to the following quotes from various governmental agencies will help keep our forests green.

United States Department of the Interior: Put cigarettes out. . . . Make sure a wood fire is out before you leave it.

United States Department of Agriculture: Fire is an ever present danger in the National Forests. Please be very careful. Build your campfire away from trees, logs, stumps, overhanging branches, dense dry grass and forest litter. Clear a 10 foot fire circle to bare soil, then dig a shallow fire pit in the center. Please locate your camp at least 100 feet away from any lake or stream to prevent pollution. Never leave a campfire unattended, even for a moment. ALWAYS BE CERTAIN YOUR FIRE IS DEAD OUT WHEN YOU LEAVE. Abandoned campfires cause many forest fires.

Please be careful where and when you smoke. NEVER smoke while walking thru the woods. Fireworks and/or explosives are illegal and not allowed. Remember if you start a fire accidentally or otherwise, the liability for damage and cost of putting out the fire can be yours. So, do help us keep the Forests and Parks beautifully green for the enjoyment of all. . . .

Open fires are prohibited above 3,500 feet in wilderness areas.

Washington State Department of Natural Resources: Beach fires can be a great part of going to the beach. However, please realize that driftwood fires are a genuine concern to firefighters and local residents on neighboring uplands. Because of these dangers, beach fires are possible only under strictly controlled circumstances.

Usually a campfire or bonfire is legal without a burning permit, if: the fire is less than 4' in diameter; you have a shovel nearby; the surrounding area is free of flammable materials; the fire is at least 50' from any structure; you leave the fire thoroughly dead.

If you do not know the local fire rules, check with the local fire district before starting a fire. Beach fires may be illegal in the district, or outdoor burning may be prohibited because of extreme fire danger or air pollution episodes.

Remember, you are legally responsible for any fire damage you cause. To report a fire, call the Department of Natural Resources fire hot line, 1-800-562-6010.

BACKCOUNTRY USE PERMITS

Backcountry use permits are required for overnight travel in the Olympic National Park. They may be obtained at ranger stations.

GOLDEN EAGLE AND GOLDEN AGE PASSPORTS

The Golden Eagle Passport allows you usage of any park managed by the federal government. It may be purchased at any park or forest service office.

The Golden Age Passport admits you free to any national park and allows you to pay half price at any national park or forest service campground where fees are charged. The Golden Age Passport is issued free to any citizen or permanent resident of the U.S. 62 years of age or older.

ORVS

Regarding ORV permits and fees please write Interagency Committee for Outdoor Recreation, 4800 Capitol Boulevard, KP-11, Tumwater, Washington 98504-5611 and request *Washington Off-Road Vehicle Guide, A Reference for ORV Enthusiasts.* This useful booklet also covers ORVs in the backcountry, off-road opportunities, places to off-road, off-roading safety and ORV volunteers.

TRILLIUMS

Trilliums bloom from late March to late May. If it is picked it will not bloom again for three to five years. Please do not pick any wildflowers.

MOUNTAIN CLIMBERS

Make sure you have good boots, a helmet, an ice ax and the ten essentials--extra food, extra clothing, candle, compass, first aid kit, flashlight, sunglasses and cream, knife and map.

DANGEROUS FALLS AND RAPIDS

The rivers emptying into Hood Canal have dangerous falls and rapids.

HIKERS

Always have rain gear, adequate clothing, good boots, food, backpacking equipment, and the ten essentials.

ANCHORING

Anchoring is one of the most important skills required for successful cruising. Chapman has an excellent chapter on anchoring and I would also recommend *The Complete Book of Anchoring and Mooring*, Earl Hinz, Maritime Press.

MARINE WEATHER SERVICES

A continuous marine weather report is broadcast to your marine VHF radio on 162.55, 162.475, or 162.40 MHz.

HYPOTHERMIA

Hypothermia is a lowering of the core body temperature to a level which could result in death. Hypothermia is possible on land in the 40 to 50 degree Fahrenheit (4 to 10 degree Celsius) range under certain conditions of wind, rain and wetness of the individual. It can also occur very rapidly in Pacific Northwest waters when a person falls overboard.

SEARCH AND RESCUE

The Coast Guard and their volunteer organization, the Coast Guard Auxiliary are among the finest in the world. A distress call is made using VHF Channel 16.

Mountain rescue is available through contacting a responsible agency such as the National Park Service who will then usually contact Olympic Mountain Rescue in Bremerton, Washington.

PRIVATE PROPERTY

The utmost respect should be shown for private property. No trespassing signs should be obeyed. If you wish to come ashore on property you suspect is private you should seek out its owner or caretaker. If you are respectful of the other persons rights I have almost always found my wishes granted and many times made a new friend.

FOULWEATHER GEAR

No matter what time of the year in the Pacific Northwest it is not always possible to avoid the rain. It is possible, however, to remain dry and warm if you own quality foulweather gear. The old saying "you get what you pay for" could not be more applicable to foulweather gear.

WEATHER AND SEA CONDITIONS

I would like to quote selected passages from the *United States Coast Pilot 7* regarding weather and sea conditions on Hood Canal:

The tidal currents in Hood Canal at times attain velocities exceeding 1.5 knots. In some places in the canal the currents are too weak and variable to predict. At times there are heavy tide rips N of and around Foulweather Bluff, sufficiently heavy to be dangerous to small boats and to break up log rafts. This is most pronounced when the ebb current from the main body of Puget Sound meets that from Hood Canal off the point, and particularly so with the ebb against a strong N or NW wind. . . . At times SW winds from Hood Canal and N winds from Dabob Bay cause a chop dangerous for small boats. Under these conditions smoother water is found near either shore.

Winds and Visibility.-Puget Sound is open to the N and S and protected to the W and E by mountains. Winds are mainly SE through SW from September through April and NW through N in late spring and summer. However, winter directions are still common in summer, as are summer directions in winter. From fall through spring, lows moving through or near the Puget Sound are responsible for the mainly S flow. Intense storms can generate sustained winds of 40 knots with 50-knot gusts over the area. These strong winds are almost always from a S direction. In the Seattle area, sustained winds of 56 knots and gusts of 60 knots have been recorded. Winds are strongest in winter and early spring, on the average. Also calm conditions are frequent in fall and winter, reflecting the lull between storm passages. In late spring and summer, winds flow into Puget Sound from the Pacific High. Often, winds are light and variable at night, then pick up to 8 to 15 knots during the afternoon, reflecting a sea breeze effect over the sound. Occasionally, a low or front will bring a return to a S flow during the summer, and these winds remain the strongest, on the average.

Fog in the Puget Sound area causes visibility problems on about 25 to 40 days each year. It most likely hinders navigation in autumn and again during January and February. This fog is mainly a land type that forms on cool, clear, calm nights, drifts out over the water, then dissipates during the day. It can hang on for several days if a stagnant condition develops. Fog can form in any month, but is least likely during April and May.

Poor visibilities are encountered more often N and S of Puget Sound than in the sound itself. In Admiralty Inlet, fog signals at Point Wilson and Double Bluff and Point No Point blow about 8 to 15 percent of the time, during the late summer and fall. Fog lowers visibilities on this part of the coast to less than 0.5 mile on about 4 to 8 days per month. South of Point Robinson, in the East Passage, the fog signals operate about 8 to 15 percent of the time in fall and midwinter. In Puget Sound, fog signals, even during the heart of the season, blow less than 8 percent of the time; less than 5 percent in Elliot Bay. Waters of Point Wells and Point Pully are among the most fog free in the area; fog signals there operate just a few hours a month for most of the year. In the Seattle area, visibility falls below 0.5 mile on about 3 to 6 days per month during the foggy season.

NAVIGATION REGULATIONS

Areas of Hood Canal are subject to regulation because of their use by the Navy. Please consult your chart and the *United States Coast Pilot 7*.

COMMON COURTESIES AND GOOD IDEAS

The following common courtesies if followed will greatly add to everyones enjoyment of Hood Canal: Be extremely careful with fire, matches and cigarettes; fire regulations apply; Do not pick flowers or damage trees or shrubs; Dispose of refuse and other garbage in containers provided for this purpose; Thoughtful boaters never dump anything over the side; Plastic litter bags are available free of charge at some parks; Park floats and wharves are intended to make landing safer and easier; Don't "hog" these facilities; Don't operate generators or other noisy machinery after dusk or before sunrise; Don't water-ski in anchorages; Don't operate motor-equipped tenders recklessly or at high speed; Do keep an eye on your boats wake; Serious damage or injuries can be caused by unnecessary wakes; Don't flush your heads where people are swimming; Don't disturb the peace and quiet of the park environment; Keep pets on a leash; Remember that firearms and fireworks are prohibited in camps and parks; Do not tempt four-footed or two-footed night visitors; Keep your valuables and ice chest locked in your car; Don't collect dead and downed firewood at parks; It adds nutrients to the soil; Alcoholic beverages may be consumed only in designated areas and kegs are prohibited at state parks; Stay on trails, shortcuts cause erosion; Uphill hiker has right of way over downhill hiker.

Chapter 3

PAST TO PRESENT

The early history of Hood Canal plays a part in one of the major events of recorded history and two of its greatest seamen and explorers are involved.

THE NOOTKA CONFLICT AND THE NORTHWEST PASSAGE

In 1789 Spain seized control of English property, ships, and men, at the main Pacific Northwest port of Nootka on the west side of Vancouver Island.

As a show of force the Spanish Government sent three ships to the Pacific Northwest to "explore, erect forts, get along with natives", and prevent the encroachment of foreigners.

The English government was incensed. Captain George Vancouver had been readying his ship *Discovery* and armed tender *Chatham* for an exploration of the Northwest to find the Northwest Passage connecting the Pacific and Atlantic Oceans which Spain, France, Portugal and England had searched for previously. Now he was given the added challenge of solving the Nootka conflict.

Captain Vancouver sailed from England January 26, 1791 arriving in northwestern waters in April of 1792. An ironic twist of destiny as we shall later see was the meeting of Captain Vancouver and the U.S. Explorer Captain Gray off the coast of Washington. Captain Gray told Captain Vancouver's Lieutenant Puget he was sailing south to explore colored water which he had seen on his way north and he believed a great river entered the ocean here. He was assured by Lieutenant Puget they too had seen this, but it was not a river. Captain Gray and his small sloop continued south and discovered and explored the Columbia River. Captain Vancouver sailed north deciding to intimidate his Spanish counterpart at Nootka and keep him waiting. Vancouver then proceeded to explore. First he explored the Strait of Juan de Fuca, headed south to explore Puget Sound and Hood Canal and then north to explore the Strait of Georgia. The following is Vancouver's original journal account of his exploration of Hood Canal:

> The wind blowing strong from the southward so much retarded our progress, that at noon we had only reached the N. W. point of the arm we had been steering for, and which was not more than five miles from our station in Oak cove, in a direction, S. 14 E.; its observed latitude was 47 degrees 53 minutes, longitude 237 degrees 36 minutes, Foulweather bluff forming the opposite point of entrance into the arm, bore east about half a league distant. The strength of the ebb tide obliged us to stop near two hours, and from its rapidity we were induced to believe, as we had before suspected, that either the eastern shore was an island, or that the tide had extensive inland communication.
>
> On the flood returning, we resumed our route, and found our supposed high round island connected with the main by a low sandy neck of land, nearly occupied by a salt-water swamp. Into the bay, formed between this point and that we had departed from, descended a few small streams of fresh water; with which, so far as we were enabled to judge, the country did not abound. This opinion was sanctioned by the Indians who visited us this

morning, bringing with them small square boxes filled with fresh water, which we could not tempt them to dispose of. Hence this branch of the inlet takes a direction about S. W. 1/2 S. near 13 miles, and is in general about half a league wide. Its shores exhibited by no means the luxuriant appearance we had left behind, being nearly destitute of the open verdant spots, and alternately composed of sandy or rocky cliffs falling abruptly into the sea, or terminating on a beach; whilst in some places the even land extended from the water side, with little or no elevation. The low projecting points cause the coast to be somewhat indented with small bays, where, near the shore, we had soundings from five to twelve fathoms; but in the middle of the channel, though not more than two miles in width, no bottom could be reached with 110 fathoms of line.

We had not advanced more than two or three miles before we lost the advantage of the flood tide, and met a stream that ran constantly down. This, with a very fresh S. W. wind, so retarded our progress, that it was not until Friday the 11th at noon that we reached the extent above mentioned, which we found to be situated due south of our observatory in port Discovery, in the latitude of 47 degrees 39 minutes. From this station, which I called HAZEL POINT in consequence of its producing many of those trees, the channel divides into two branches, one taking a direction nearly due north, the other S. W. We still continued on the right hand, or continental shore, and found the northern arm terminate at the distance of about seven miles in a spacious bason, where bottom could not be found with 70 fathoms of line. As we returned to take up our abode for the night at the S. W. point of this arm, we observed some smoke on shore, and saw a canoe hauled up into a small creek; but none of the inhabitants could be discovered, nor did we hear or see any thing of them during the night.

The next morning, Saturday the 12th, at four o'clock, we again embarked. Having been supplied for five days only, our provisions were greatly exhausted, and the commencement of this, which was the sixth, threatened us with short allowance. Our sportsmen had been unable to assist our stock; and the prospect of obtaining any supplies from the natives was equally uncertain. The region we had lately passed seemed nearly destitute of human beings. The brute creation also had deserted the shores; the tracks of deer were no longer to be seen; nor was there an aquatic bird on the whole extent of the canal; animated nature seemed nearly exhausted; and her awful silence was only now and then interrupted by the croaking of a raven, the breathing of a seal, or the scream of an eagle. Even these solitary sounds were so seldom heard, that the rustling of the breeze along the shore, assisted by the solemn stillness that prevailed, gave rise to ridiculous suspicions in our seamen of hearing rattlesnakes, and other hideous monsters, in the wilderness, which was composed of the productions already mentioned, but which appeared to grow with infinitely less vigour than we had been accustomed to witness.

To the westward and N. W. lay that range of snowy mountains, noticed the morning we spoke with the *Columbia*. These gradually descended in a southern direction, whilst the summit of the eastern range now and then appearing, seemed to give bounds to this low country on that side. Between the S. E. and S. W. a country of a very moderate height seemed to extend as far as the eye could reach; and, from its eminences and vallies, there was reason to believe that this inlet continued to meander a very considerable distance, which made me much regret that we were not provided for a longer excursion. Yet, having proceeded thus far, I resolved to continue our researches, though at the expense of a little hunger, until the inlet should either terminate, or so extensively open, as to render it expedient that the vessels should be brought up; which would be a very tedious and disagreeable operation, in consequence of the narrowness of the channel, and the great depth of the water.

Soundings in some places only could be gained close to the shore; and in the middle no bottom had anywhere been found with 100 fathoms of line, although the shores were in general low, and not half a league asunder.

Having very pleasant weather, and a gentle favorable breeze, we proceeded, and passed several runs of fresh water. Near one of the largest we observed our latitude at noon to be 47 degrees 27 minutes; and once again had the pleasure of approaching an inhabited country. A canoe, in which there were three men, went alongside the launch, and bartered a few trifles for beads, iron, and copper, but declined every invitation from us to come on shore. From Mr. Puget I learned, that they appeared to be very honest in their dealings, and had used their utmost endeavors to prevail on the party in the launch to attend them home, which he understood to be at the distance of about a league, and for which they seemed to make the best of their way, probably to acquaint their friends with the approach of strangers. Soon after we had dined, a smoke was observed near the supposed place of their residence; made, as we concluded, for the purpose of directing us to their habitations, for which we immediately set off, agreeably to their very civil invitation.

An idea during this excursion had occurred to us, that part of the brute creation have an aversion to the absence of the human race; this opinion seemed now in some measure confirmed, by the appearance for the first time during the last three days, of several species of ducks, and other aquatic birds. I do not, however, mean absolutely to infer, that it is the affection of the lower orders of the creation to man, that draws them to the same spots which human beings prefer, since it is highly probable that such places as afford the most eligible residence in point of sustenance to the human race, in an uncivilized state, may be, by the brute creation, resorted to for the same purpose.

The habitations of our new friends appeared to be situated nearly at the extremity of this inlet, or where it appeared to take a very sharp turn to the S. E. still favoring our hopes of returning by the great eastern arm. These, however, vanished on landing, as we found its S. W. direction terminate in land, apparently low and swampy, with a shoal extending some distance from its shores, forming a narrow passage to the south-eastward into a cove or bason, which seemed its termination also in that direction.

Here we found the finest stream of fresh water we had yet seen; from the size, clearness, and rapidity of which, little doubt could be entertained of its having its source in perpetual springs. Near it were two miserable huts with mats thrown carelessly over them, protecting their tenants neither from the heat nor severity of the weather; these huts seemed calculated to contain only the five or six men then present, though previously to our quitting the boats we supposed a greater number of persons had been seen; those were probably their women, who on our approach had retired to the woods.

These good people conducted themselves in the most friendly manner. They had little to dispose of, yet they bartered away their bows and arrows without the least hesitation, together with some small fish, cockles, and clams; of the latter we purchased a large quantity, a supply of which was very acceptable in the low condition of our stock. They made us clearly to understand, that in the cove to the S. E. we should find a number of their countrymen, who had the like commodities to dispose of; and being anxious to leave no doubt concerning a further inland navigation by this arm of the sea, and wishing to establish, as far as possible, a friendly intercourse with the inhabitants of the country, which, from the docile and inoffensive manners of those we had seen, appeared a task of no great difficulty, we proceeded to a low point of land that forms the north entrance into the cove. There we beheld a number of natives, who did not betray the smallest apprehension at our approach; the whole assembly remained quietly seated on the grass, excepting two or three whose particular office seemed to be that of making us welcome to their country. These presented us with some fish, and received in return trinkets of various kinds, which delighted them excessively. They attended us to their companions, who amounted in number to about sixty, including the women and children. We were received by them with equal cordiality, and treated with marks of great friendship and hospitality. A short time was here employed in exchanges of mutual civilities. The females on this occasion took a very active part. They presented us with fish, arrows, and other trifles, in a way that convinced us they had much pleasure in so doing. They did not appear to differ in any respect from the inhabitants we had before seen; and some of our gentlemen were of opinion that they recognized the persons of one or two who had visited us on the preceding Thursday morning; particularly one man, who had suffered very much from the small pox. This deplorable disease is not only common, but it is greatly to be apprehended is very fatal amongst them, as its indelible marks were seen on many; and several had lost the sight of one eye, which was remarked to be generally the left, owing most likely to the virulent effects of this baneful disorder. The residence of these people here was doubtless of a temporary nature; few had taken the trouble of erecting their usual miserable huts, being content to lodge on the ground, with loose mats only for their covering.

From this point, which is situated nearly at the south extremity of the channel in latitude 47 degrees 21 minutes, longitude 237 degrees 6 1/2 minutes, little doubt existed of the cove terminating its navigation. To ascertain this, whilst I remained with these civil people, Mr. Johnstone was directed to row round the projection that had obstructed our view of the whole circumference of the cove, which is about two miles; and, if it were not closed, to pursue its examination. Our former conjectures being confirmed, on his return we prepared to depart; and, as we were putting off from the shore, a cloak of inferior sea otter skins was brought down, which I purchased for a small piece of copper. Upon this they made signs that if we would remain, more, and of a superior quality, should be produced; but as this was not our object, and as we had finished our proposed talk sooner than was expected this morning, to the no small satisfaction of our whole party, we directed our course back towards port Discovery, from which we were now about 70 miles distant.

A fresh northwardly wind, and the approach of night, obliged us to take up our abode about two miles from the Indians, some of whom had followed us along the beach until we landed, when they posted themselves at the distance of about half a mile, to observe our different employments; at dark they all retired, and we neither heard nor saw any thing more of them. The rise and fall of the tide, although the current constantly ran down without any great degree of rapidity, appeared to have been nearly ten feet, and it was high water 3h 50' after the moon passed the meridian.

Early on Sunday morning the 13th, we again embarked; directing our route down the inlet, which, after the Right Honorable Lord Hood, I called HOOD'S CHANNEL; but our progress homeward was so very slow, that it was Monday afternoon, the 14th, before we reached Foulweather bluff. This promontory is not ill named, for we had scarcely landed, when a heavy rain commenced, which continuing the rest of the day, obliged us to remain stationary. This detention I endeavoured to reconcile with the hope that the next morning would permit some examination, or at least afford us a view of the great eastern arm, before we returned to the ships; but in this I was disappointed. After waiting until ten o'clock in the forenoon of Tuesday the 15th, without the least prospect of an alteration for the better, we again set out with a fresh breeze at S. S. E. attended with heavy squalls and torrents of rain; and about four in the afternoon arrived on board, much to the satisfaction I believe of all parties, as great anxiety had been enter-

tained for our safety, in consequence of the unex-
pected length of our absence. The swivels fired
from our boat and that of the *Chatham's* the
morning after our departure, were heard on board,
and were the cause of much alarm after the expi-
ration of the time appointed for our return.

At the close of the summer Captain Vancouver still
had not found his long sought Northwest Passage and
set sail for Nootka where the Spanish Explorer Senor
Don Juan Francisco de la Bodega y Quadra became his
close friend even though they were unable to reach an
agreement regarding the Nootka conflict.

THE HUDSON BAY COMPANY

The years following Captain Vancouver's departure
saw only the presence of Hudson Bay Company fur
trappers on Hood Canal. There were two Hudson Bay
Company outposts to serve them on Hood Canal--a
blockhouse at Union and a larger outpost and garrison
at Seabeck.

THE WILKES EXPEDITION AND THE OREGON TERRITORY

The Wilkes Expedition of 1826 paved the way for the
pioneers and settlers of the Hood Canal area. U.S.
Secretary of the Navy gave orders for the expedition to
"survey and examine the territory of the United States
on the northwest coast, Columbia River and along to
San Francisco." The Wilkes Expedition in carrying out
these orders explored the interior of the Hood Canal
area.

When the Oregon Territory was formed by an Act of
Congress in 1848 the time was right for the settlement
of the Hood Canal area. It is interesting to reflect how
the course of history could have been changed had
Captain Vancouver been the one to discover the
Columbia River and not the U.S. Explorer Captain Gray.
The discovery of the Columbia River was our main
claim to the Oregon Territory in spite of a predominant
English presence through the Hudson Bay Company.

HOMESTEADERS AND LUMBER

Around 1853 homesteaders started coming to the Hood Canal area. They came across the plains in covered wagons and around the Horn by sailing ship. They were all looking for the haven of their dreams-their own land.

Also around this time the Pope and Talbot Company built a sawmill at Port Gamble. Captain Talbot upon seeing the virgin forests of the Hood Canal area remarked there was, "Timber!, timber!, till you can't sleep." Later a mill was built at Seabeck. These mill towns were autonomous commercial centers with their own company store, which supplied the loggers, mill workers, sailors, homesteaders, and neighboring Indians with necessities and luxuries. They could also outfit the ships which carried their cut lumber to all parts of the world--Hawaii, Japan, China, New Zealand, Australia, South America, Europe, and the Eastern seaboard. Seabeck had its own shipyard which was considered the most modern in the world. It built ships to move its lumber such as the *Cassandra Adams* which could carry 1,000,000 feet of lumber.

The homesteaders had a hard life and often their homesteads couldn't support their families and they worked at mill company camps logging or directly for the mill. The following quote from *With Pride In Heritage* (Port Townsend: Jefferson County Historical Society, 1966, 172) shows the hardness of life and the close dependence of homesteaders and lumber:

> The pioneer women who lived up the rivers often fought the lands and wilds alone while their men worked in these logging camps for cash needed to buy flour, salt, ammunition, and the tools for homesteading. The five or six miles to their homes upriver was too far to walk after working 12 hours in the woods so they stayed in the camps while the women tended gardens, milked and herded cows, fed chickens, and kept the dearly cleared land from reverting back to jungle. On Saturday nights they hiked the miles up the lonely valleys to their homesteads carrying provisions on their backs.

It is not surprising that many left when employment was offered elsewhere, if only to be closer to their families, but the rich bottom land, the virgin timber, the beauty of the area itself always lured another to take the place of one who left, and a cabin never stood empty long.

The quote ends on a positive note and shows why the area was eventually tamed. Today the descendants of some of the early pioneers still farm the same land, and some work for the Pope and Talbot mill, which is the oldest continually operating lumber mill in the United States.

FISHING AND SHELLFISH

Fishing and shellfish harvesting played a vital role in the economic survival of the early pioneers on Hood Canal. This was especially true for the Scandinavian pioneers who settled the eastern side of the canal. Hood Canal reminded them of their native countries where they also had earned their living from the sea. They gave their communities Scandinavian names such as Breidablik and Vinland.

The following recollections from *Kitsap County History* (Silverdale: Kitsap County Historical Society, 1977) show fishings importance:

Father knew how to make gill nets so it wasn't long before we had one made to catch salmon. We used to go down to Hood Canal in the evening with the net and anchor one end to shore and anchor the other end straight out from shore. In the morning we would go down again and pack home our fish. Sometime the seal would beat us to the salmon but as a rule there would be plenty left for us. We also had a purse seine to catch herring and one end was held on shore and the other end was carried around on a boat till both ends came together. Then we pulled the seine in with more herring than we could use. At that time there wasn't anybody that worried about conservation of anything. When the fish traps were in full operation all along the Canal and if the canneries were not able to take care of all the fish they just turned the fish loose because there were plenty more to catch even if most of the fish turned loose died.

The Senior Pfundt's son Albert purchased property in Holly in 1894 and married Nellie Wyatt. He was a fisherman, purseseiner and shrimper and sold salmon to Holly residents for 5 cents each.

Fred Pfundt supported the family by sending salmon, cod, shrimp and octopi to the Seattle markets. Octopi and shrimp sold for much higher prices than salmon; at 10 cents and 6 cents a pound respectively. At one time the shrimp fishermen went on strike, including Fred, when the buyer said he would pay no more than 3 cents a pound for shrimp. In the early years, fish were sold at Union City.

In 1909 there were oyster lands on Holly Bay, south of Nellita with a claim registered to P. H. Hunter and A. M. Fredson, and the Big Beef Creek Bay.

One morning in September 1914 the natives of Bangor were very much surprised and startled to see a small village on floats which had been towed in during the night. Upon investigation it was found that the clam cannery from Union City at the head of Hood's Canal, had been moved to its new location where it continued to operate for some time. When going at its full capacity, it could handle 250 bushels of clams per day and employed 24 women and six men.

The clam cannery is long gone and the salmon are drastically reduced in number, but Hood Canal residents, some related to early pioneers, are still making a living from the sea. Hood Canal's shrimp, salmon, herring, Geoduck's (large clams), and Pacific Oyster's now supply world markets.

TRANSPORTATION

The history of transportation in the Hood Canal area is interesting because, for many years the only means of transportation was by water. The earliest form of transportation was by rowboat. Many of the early pioneers came from Seattle by rowboat, the trip taking up to four days. An improvement over this type of transportation was the sloop. Ed Clayson had a small sloop which carried mail, people, and supplies between Seabeck and Port Gamble and, depending on the wind, could make the 80 mile round trip in a week. Then came the wood and coal powered steamers. The most well known, the *Perdita*, could make the round trip between Seattle and the ports of call on Hood Canal in a day. Passengers and freight were carried. The freight could be a cow and when it arrived at its port was shoved through a deck door to swim ashore.

The railroad also played a vital part in Hood Canal's development. On the northern end of the canal the Port Townsend Southern Railroad ran as far south as Quilcene with plans to run south to its union with the rail line from Portland. On the southern end of the canal the Union Pacific Railroad was to make Union its saltwater terminal and let men and supplies off at Union to start building the line to Olympia. All this railroad activity and speculation led to towns all up and down the canal coming into existence many of which are still there today. But the Great Baring Bras Bank Failure in London, England started the panic of 1893 when everybody went broke resulting in these lines never being built.

Eventually the steamers were replaced by roads, ferryboats and even a floating bridge.

RECREATION

The early history of the canal deserves an account of recreation. As today, many people came to Hood Canal's resorts to relax and enjoy themselves. Perhaps the most well-known was the luxurious resort called the Antlers on Lake Cushman. Lake Cushmans trout fishing was world famous and people were also taken on packtrains into the interior of the beautiful Olympic Mountains. The original Pierce Ranch Homestead was turned into a summer resort in 1910 with a dance pavilion, tents for the guests to stay in, home cooking, laundry maid, vegetable garden, caretaker and dairy barn worker. It ran as such for 20 years. Alderwood Resort was another famous resort complete with luxury cottages on the canal, still in use, and an 8 hole golf course, now expanded to 18.

Well-known on the other side of the canal was the resort run by Albert Pfundt at Holly. He rented out summer cottages right on the shore, with beautiful views of the canal, Mt. Constance and the Brothers and little kicker boats for salmon fishing.

Little has changed since those early days except the numbers of people and more modern facilities and concessions. The reason people come to the canal is still the same--the natural beauty of the canal and its many recreational activities.

Page 46 Top

John McReavy house and store. (Courtesy of the Washington State Historical Society, Tacoma, Washington, photo no. 5580, Asahel Curtis Collection)

Page 46 Bottom

Potlatch, booming grounds in foreground. (Courtesy of the Washington State Historical Society, Tacoma, Washington, photo no. 5572, Asahel Curtis Collection)

Page 47 Top

Logging, Hoodsport. (Courtesy of the Washington State Historical Society, Tacoma, Washington, photo no. 5786A, Asahel Curtis Collection)

Page 47 Bottom

Logging, Hoodsport. (Courtesy of the Washington State Historical Society, Tacoma, Washington, photo no. 5786B, Asahel Curtis Collection)

Page 48

Lumbermill, Port Gamble. (Courtesy of the Washington State Historical Society, Tacoma, Washington, photo no. 4795, Asahel Curtis Collection)

Page 49 Top

Dosewallips River, tent camping. (Courtesy of the Washington State Historical Society, Tacoma, Washington, photo no. 47295, Asahel Curtis Collection)

Page 49 Center

The Antlers, Lake Cushman. (Courtesy of the Washington State Historical Society, Tacoma, Washington, photo no. 8751, Asahel Curtis Collection)

Page 49 Bottom

Alderbrook Resort. (Courtesy of the Washington State Historical Society, Tacoma, Washington, photo no. 59558, Asahel Curtis Collection)

Page 50 Top

Brinnon homestead. (Courtesy of the Washington State Historical Society, Tacoma, Washington, photo no. 5803, Asahel Curtis Collection)

Page 50 Bottom

Pierce Ranch. (Courtesy of the Washington State Historical Society, Tacoma, Washington, photo no. 5797, Asahel Curtis Collection)

Page 51 Top

Horse and buggy, Hood Canal. (Courtesy of the Washington State Historical Society, Tacoma, Washington, photo no. 5565, Asahel Curtis Collection)

Page 51 Bottom

Virgin trees, horse and buggy, Lake Cushman Road. (Courtesy of the Washington State Historical Society, Tacoma, Washington, photo no. 5799, Asahel Curtis Collection)

Page 52 Top

S.S. Perdita, Hood Canal. (Courtesy of the Washington State Historical Society, Tacoma, Washington, photo no. 5567, Asahel Curtis Collection)

Page 52 Bottom

Indian encampment, fishing boat, Pleasant Harbor. (Courtesy of the Washington State Historical Society, Tacoma, Washington, photo no. 5806, Asahel Curtis Collection)

Chapter 4

NATIVE HERITAGE

No one really knows the origins of the Pacific Coast Indians. Philip Drucker, a respected anthropologist, believes at the end of the ice age, about ten thousand years ago, a fishing and hunting people from Northern Asia came across the Bering Strait ice bridge and extended their influence to California. He believes these primitive people mingled with Indians who migrated out of the mountainous hinterlands to become the coast Indians.

FIRST INHABITANTS

The coast Indians lived from Alaska to Northern California. Anthropologists prefer to differentiate the coast Indians on the basis of language and not tribe or nation. From the north to the south the coast people and the territory they occupied are as follows:

Tlingit. Southeastern Alaska from Yakutat Bay to the mouth of Portland Inlet.

Haida. The Queen Charlotte Islands and, in late prehistoric times, southern Prince of Wales Island.

Tsimshian. The lower reaches of the Nass and Skeena Rivers and the coast from Portland Inlet to Milbanke Sound.

Northern Kwakiutl.   Milbanke Sound to Rivers Inlet.

Southern Kwakiutl.   Rivers Inlet to Salmon River on Vancouver Island and the upper reaches of Douglas Channel and Gardner Canal.

Bella Coola.   The upper reaches of Dean and Burke Channels.

Westcoast (Nootkan).   The west coast of Vancouver Island from Cape Cook to Port Renfrew.

Coast Salish.   The Strait of Georgia from Campbell River to and including Puget Sound and Hood Canal.

The groups above could also be broken down into separate groups based on dialects and territory. The Salish group was composed of eleven separate tribes. One of these tribes was the Too-an-hooch or Tu-ad-hu, now called Twana, who occupied both sides of Hood Canal for its entire length.

SEAGOING CULTURE

The coast Indians developed the most advanced culture in North America outside of Mexico. The mild climate, together with a constant rainfall, sustained a rich forest which provided most of their material needs. The sea though was what made the coast Indians culture unique. They built their permanent villages on riverbanks or protected coves and in summer traveled in their canoes to their salmon fishing grounds. The over abundance of salmon and other sea resources enabled the coast Indians to live free of want, and have leisure time which could be devoted to other pursuits such as travel, religion and social events. Never before had a primitive culture been able to advance this far without an agricultural base.

HOUSING

The Coast Salish were noted for their potlatch houses and mat houses. The following quote from *The Notebooks of Myron Eells* gives us an excellent description:

The potlatch houses. These are the only public buildings among the Indians. They are not always built on a uniform plan. One was built on the Skokomish reservation in 1875-76, which was about 40 by 200 feet. . . .Large tamahnous posts about 9 feet long, from 1 1/2 to 2 1/4 feet wide and 5 or 6 inches thick, support the sides of the building. Smaller posts support the cone of the roof. A platform for beds about 3 1/2 feet wide and 2 feet above the ground, runs entirely around the inside of the building. A kind of shelf is overhead for storing various articles.

Small walls are made, one on each side of the doors, to keep the wind and cold from making the bed platforms too uncomfortable, and they often serve to divide the people who come from different localities from each other. Low seats, about 6 inches high, are made in front of the bed-platform, on which also their beds are sometimes spread. Fires are made in front of these seats. Occasionally a post extends from the ground to the ridge pole to support the latter. Large round cross beams, considerably larger in the middle than at each end, extend from one side of the house to the other, resting on the top of the large posts, and on these are placed most of the posts which support the ridge pole. There are three doors on the front side facing the water, one at ech end, and none at the back, which is against a hill.

One built by the Twana Indians about 1868 was similar to the one just described, but larger, having been about 50 by 300 feet. . . .The one just described so fully was used for potlatches in 1876, and again in 1878, but was afterwards crushed by the snow and destroyed.

The summer house or mat house. These are made of mats, with occasionally a few boards. Generally they are built at fishing places during the summer. Inside, the beds are laid around the side on boards a few inches from the ground. The fire is in the middle; most of the space overhead is occupied with fish which are being dried. People and things are stowed where any room can be found, and the whole atmosphere is filled with smoke.

FOOD GATHERING

Salmon was the staple food of the Twana Indians and was supplemented by cod, halibut, herring, trout and a small oily member of the smelt family called eulachon ('hoo-li-gan). The sea also provided seaweed, seals, and all manner of shellfish. When the Twana Indians grew tired of seafood they could hunt deer and bear. The land also provided numerous types of berries, edible roots, birds and eggs.

Salmon were caught by nets, gaffs, harpoons and weirs--a cedar stake fence built in a river to catch or trap fish. The Twana also used a seine or reef net at the mouths of their rivers. It was operated between two canoes and was made of twined cedar bark or spun nettle fibres. Cod, trout, and halibut were caught on plain V-shaped hooks of bent hardwood, two to a line. Lines were made from spruce roots, cedar bark or kelp stems. Cod and trout were also speared. Herring and eulachon were caught using a herring rake "comb" which was swept through the water impaling the herring on its sharp teeth. Herring and eulachon were also netted.

The plentiful deer and bear were caught using nets, pits, deadfalls and slip-loop snares. Nets made out of twigs, bark or sinew were a favorite device for entangling animals and birds. Animals were driven into strong nets set across their paths and flying waterfowl were caught at dusk by a net strung between two high poles.

Most fish and game were smoked or dried and placed in safe caches to last the winter. The eulachon, however, was most valued for its oil. (The eulachon is so oily it can be lighted like a candle and because of this is also called the candlefish). The Twana Indians would allow the fish to sit for several days and then boil them and skim the fat off the top of the water. The remainder of the oil would be obtained by pressing the fish in a basket. The Twana Indian considered this oil a delicacy and at meals would dip their food in it. The oil was also used to preserve berries and other food.

SOCIAL UNIT

The family was the basic social unit and was autonomous with its own chief. The family was made up of slaves, commoners, and noblemen. The slaves were either captured or born from captured slaves. The commoners made up the majority of the family and were not closely enough related to the founder of the family to be considered noblemen. The noblemen were few in number and directly related to the founder of the family. The noblemen had position, rank and privileges; i.e. the right to a fishing ground, song, strip of land, etc. Each family lived in its own plank house, and if it was a large family, it may have had additional houses. Originally each village came from one genealogical family, but over time due to marriage, war, and overpopulation a village contained representatives of several genealogical families. Usually a village was made up of one through five named house clusters. The chief of the most prestigious house would be in charge of the village but his leadership was very loose.

The villages in a certain geographic area were basically autonomous and their unity was based on kinship between members, a common traditional background, and their own self interest; i.e. protecting each other against outside hostile Indians.

The Twana Indians lived at three villages--the Du-hle-lips, who lived at the head of Hood Canal; the Skokomish who lived near the mouth of the Skokomish River; and the Quilceeds or Kol-ceedobish who lived around the Quilceed Bay and mouth of the Duk-a-boos and Dos-wail-opsh Rivers.

POTLATCH

The Twana Indians did not live in isolation and visited other groups to trade, socialize, or attend a potlatch. Occasionally they went to war against another group to get slaves, property, or avenge a slight, but mainly the Twanas were a peace loving people.

A potlatch was a ceremony given by a chief and his group to another group of Indians. The chief would give away gifts and other chiefs and Indians would accept the gifts. Everything was controlled by a rigid protocol; i.e. seating, issuing of invitations, serving of food, and the order and content of speeches, songs and dances. These potlatches could go on for days and by the end of the potlatch the chief would have given away everything he owned but he would possess new rights and privileges because of the potlatch. As an example, if the chiefs father had died the chief would give a potlatch in honor of his deceased fathers spirit. The acceptance of gifts by those present would indicate they now accepted the new chief and all the rights and privileges passed down to him because of his fathers death, such as the right to his fathers fishing grounds. There was much competition between chiefs over who could give the best potlatch and at the next potlatch the chief was invited to he might receive more than he had previously given away.

RELIGION

The coast Indians didn't believe in a heaven. Their myths talk about a world above inhabited by immortals into which some of their people had climbed. They did know of a deity linked with the sky or sun but this deity was remote or vague and of little importance in their daily routine. Philip Drucker writes in *Cultures of the North Pacific Coast* (New York: Harper & Row, Publishers, Inc., 1965, 84):

> More important to the Indians were the supernatural beings who inhabited their own world: the forests, the mountains, the beaches, the waters and the nearer reaches of the skies. These were the gods with whom human beings might come in contact, to their benefit or disaster. A great many of these were guardian spirits, familiar to most American Indians--beings who could confer blessings, good fortune, and even a measure of supernatural power on man. Many were animal spirits, at least they assumed the form of animals; others were monsters of weird and terrifying aspect. It seems that monsters were more numerous on the North Pacific coast than in other parts of western North

America. There were huge cave-dwelling man-eating birds with tremendous sharp beaks; there were frightful sea monsters in the ocean deeps. On the highest mountain peaks dwelled thunderbirds, who kept live whales as easily as an eagle flies away with a trout in its talons. Ogres and malevolent dwarfs shared the forest with animals and animal spirits. A huge hand emerged from the ground, shaking a rattle, but no one dared to imagine to what horrendous form it was attached. Giant quartz crystals possessed a life of their own; they glowed with a blinding white light, vibrated with a humming sound, flew through the air, and killed ordinary men and animals with a mysterious charge. These are but a few of the myriad of terrifying supernatural beings who peopled the native environment. All were dangerous to mortals, but most of them could confer valuable gifts too.

Animal spirits of a special class were believed to live in groups similar to those of human beings. The core of this belief related to the salmon, who dwelled in a huge house, similar to the houses of the Indians, far under the sea. In their home, the salmon went about in human form. When the time came for the annual runs, they put on their robes of salmon skin and converted themselves into the fish that were the staple of the area. The run was thus conceived to be a voluntary sacrifice for the benefit of mankind, and when the bones of the fish were returned to the water, they washed down to the sea where each fish became reassembled and came back to life.

The quote by Drucker teaches us much about the Indians religion. The world to the Indian could be a dangerous place. It was critical for the Indian to be at peace with his environment and the supernatural powers who inhabited it. As the salmon legend shows, if the Indian took from the sea to live he also gave back to the sea to live.

In order to live in harmony with nature and its spirits the Indian had to be purified and seek the favor of the supernatural spirits. To do this he had to obtain his tamahnous. When a person obtained his tamahnous he could invoke its aid as his guardian spirit. The following quote from *The Notebooks of Myron Eells* shows how he obtained his tamahnous:

The story of Big John's grandfather. When he was a young man, he was sent by his father to find his tamahnous, but could not find it. Again and again he was sent, but with the same result. At one time he stayed eighteen days with nothing to eat or drink and at one time his throat was so dry, that it about stuck together. Again his father drove him off, and he went down Hood Canal along the beach, but found nothing. He then came back, and on his return, saw three young men who had eaten some poison, lying dead on the beach. Accordingly, he turned back, and as he went along, he saw a sunfish, and remembering that he had heard that one young man had found his tamahnous by eating the whole of a sunfish, except the heart, he concluded to do the same. Hence he went to work, and when he had eaten all around it, except the heart, he fell down dead, that is, his spirit left his body. His spirit was taken by the sunfish, a long way off, through a region of darkness. At last he saw a gleam of light, as it were, between two clouds. There he saw a woman singing, and although he could not hear her, as she was so far off, yet he could hear the echo of her singing behind him. She brought his spirit back to his body, and thus he obtained his tamahnous. It was very strong.

The Indian also wanted to obtain spiritual power to use: against his enemy, illness, or misfortune; in acquiring wealth; in his dancing and singing.

The quest for the highest level of spiritual power is associated with the shaman. Although there were many differences amongst the coast shamans the following quote from *The Notebooks of Myron Eells* shows the universal role they played as a person with a high degree of spiritual powers and as an intermediary between the ordinary Indian and spiritual world.

When I was at the Indian doctor's house they tamahnoused over my brother, for that is the reason my parents went to his house. First he learned what was the kind of sickness. The doctor took it and soon after that my brother, about nine or ten years old, became stiff and while I sat I heard my father say that his breath was gone. I went out, for I did not wish to see my brother lying dead before me; when I came back he was breathing just a little but his eyes were closed; the doctor was taking care of his breath with his tamahnous and waiting for more persons to come, so that there should be enough to beat on the sticks when he should tamahnous so as to learn the kind of sickness. Then he went on and saw that there was another kind of sickness besides the one he had taken out and it went over my brother and almost immediately killed him. The doctor took it and travelled (in his spirit) with another kind of tamahnous to see where my brother's spirit was; he found it at Humhummi (15 miles distant), where my parents and brother had camped in a recent journey. So my brother became better after a hard tamahnous.

The boy was cured and the shamans prestige enhanced.

LITERATURE

The literature of the Twanas consisted of a wealth of stories passed on and told by their narrators. The following quote from *The Notebooks of Myron Eells* is a good example:

They also say that a long time ago a man who lived at Union City, and was very successful in catching porpoises, had a brother who was his enemy, who lived up the river, and who tried to injure him but could not. This brother especially tried to injure him by seeking to prevent his catching porpoises, but could not. Failing in this, he made a wooden porpoise, put his tamahnous into it, and put it into the water, where he thought his brother would catch it. His brother at Union City found it, and, thinking that surely it was a porpoise, caught it; he found really that it was too strong for him and that he was caught by it, for it took him north under water to the unknown place where ducks live in summer, which is also inhabited by a race of pigmy men a foot or two high, between whom and the ducks there is war. He helped the pigmies, killed many ducks and ate some, whereupon the pigmies called him a cannibal and became enraged at him.

At last a whale caught him and brought him back nearly to Union City. He very much wished to be thrown out on dry land or in shallow water near the land. But his wish was not granted, for by some means the whale vomited him up in deep water, and he swam to land. This is the reason why the dentalia, the species of shell formerly used as money, are found in deep water, for they were vomited up with him. If his wish had been granted, and he was thrown on dry land or in shallow water, they would have been found there.

ARTIFACTS

The artifacts of the coast Indians were many and varied and considered art works of great beauty. Many of these artifacts are not subject to decay and are still being found today either accidentally or through archaeological excavation, i.e. bowls, sculptured stones, spindle whorls, pestles, combs, knives, etc.

Other artifacts are subject to decay being made from wood and other fibrous material, i.e. baskets, blankets, mats, canoes, etc.

Because of its relevance to the Twana Indians an explanation of mat making from *The Notebooks of Myron Eells* is very interesting:

This grass is cut by the women in July and August, dried in the sun, and tied in bunches, as large as can be comfortably carried. When a woman finds time to make mats, she assorts her rushes into three lots according to size. Of the longest rushes she makes the largest mats, which are about 5 feet wide and 12 to 20 feet long. Of rushes of medium length, she makes mats about 3 feet wide, and from 8 to 15 feet long. Of the smaller stalks she makes mats about 2 feet wide and from 2 to 4 feet long. The largest mats are used chiefly for lining wooden houses and in constructing mat houses. Those of medium size are used at times for the same purpose, for the half-circle camps, for beds, pillows, seats, table covers, and as substitutes for umbrellas and oil-cloth, two layers forming an almost complete protection from the rain. The narrowest mats, usually from 3 to 4 feet long, are used mostly for cushions, as in canoes, and for the paddlers to kneel on. While sorting over the rushes, she splits off a small part from the base of the stalk, of which she makes a string, which she uses in sewing the mat together.

INTO THE CORPORATE ERA

The story of the history of the Twana Indians would not be complete without telling how their contact with the white man affected them.

The first recorded contact the Twanas had with the white man was with Captain Vancouver and his party near the head of Hood Canal in May of 1792. Captain Vancouver wrote in his journal:

We had not been long out of Oak cove, when we descried some Indians paddling slowly under the lee of a rocky point, with an apparent intention of waiting our approach. In this they were soon gratified, and on our arrival, they did not seem to express the least doubt of our friendly disposition towards them. They courteously offered such things as they possessed, and cordially accepted some medals, beads, knives, and other trinkets, which I presented to them, and with which they appeared to be highly pleased.

Not much is known about their contact with the white man between Captain Vancouver's visit and 1826 when the Wilkes Expedition explored Hood Canal. They probably did see the occasional adventurer, fisherman, trapper and logger.

Around 1855 the Twana Indians life style was forever changed by the white man when they signed the Point-No-Point Treaty with the white man which created the Skokomish Reservation and moved all the Indians of Hood Canal onto the reservation who were then called the Skokomish. The following by Twana men taken from the minutes of a council held by Commissioner F. R. Brunot in September 4, 1871 shows why:

> By Big Frank, the present head chief: I am the only one who was at the treaty at Point-No-Point. I heard what Governor Stevens said, and thought it was good. I am like a white man, and think as the white man does. Governor Stevens said all the Indians would grow up and the President would make them good. He told them all the Indians would become as white men; that all their children would learn to read and write. I was glad to hear it. Governor Stevens told them, "I will go out and have the land surveyed, and it will be yours and your children's forever." I thought that very good. He said a doctor and carpenter and farmer would come. The chiefs thought that all was good, they thought the President was doing a kindness. I never spoke my mind to anyone. I talk to you, because you come from Washington. All the Agents talk differently. You talk as Governor Stevens did. I hear what you say. Every Agent who comes here, I don't know them. I thought all Governor Stevens said was very good. Perhaps the President thinks all the Indians are good, as they were to be under the treaty, but they are not. They are Indians still. I think there was plenty of money sent by the President, but I think much did not come here. Perhaps it gets scattered. I really think it does not come. When it comes it is in calico. But I know more is sent than gets here.

> By Spar, the head chief at the time, since dead: When I came here I did not know much. I was here when the reservation was opened, and know what was done. When the Agents came, they never

taught us anything, never said, "Go, and fix your places." All they think of is to steal; to sell the reservation cattle and reservation hay; to sell the fruit and get all they can; to go and log and sell them. That is all every Agent has done. They never advised us what to do, never helped us. After I had seen all this I was sorry. Did the President send men for this, to come and get what money they could out of the reservation and their pay? I know the Indians lose all their cattle. When they get the money, where does it go? When I asked about it, they say they will punish me. I thought the President did not send them for that. I got very poor and wanted to borow the reservation team. You know what I have done. They refused me the use of the cattle.

By Duke William: I am glad to see you. All our folks are very poor. Our planting grounds, and logs, and apples, and hay are taken from us, and I felt sad, and wanted to go and see the President. I know I will not live long. I asked the Indians to give me the money, and I would go and see the President. I would have gone if you had not come here. Did the President send men as Agents to log and get all the benefits? That is what I wanted to go ask the President.

As in their past the Skokomish are still fishermen, farmers, and loggers but the life of an Indian in a white man's culture is still not easy and is strewn with heartbreak and tragedy. Many believe the survival of the Skokomish Indian is going to be related to the revival of pride in their past culture of being an Indian. If this is the case the Skokomish Indians place in American Society is assured.

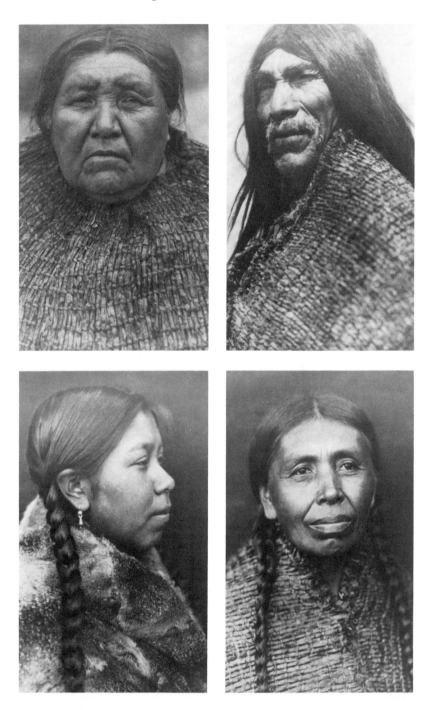

Page 68 Top Left

Quilceed Indian. (Courtesy of the Washington State Historical Society, Tacoma, Washington, photograph by Edward Curtis)

Page 68 Top Right

Quilceed Indian. (Courtesy of the Washington State Historical Society, Tacoma, Washington, photograph by Edward Curtis)

Page 68 Bottom Left

Skokomish Indian. (Courtesy of the Washington State Historical Society, Tacoma, Washington, photograph by Edward Curtis)

Page 68 Bottom Right

Skokomish Indian. (Courtesy of the Washington State Historical Society, Tacoma, Washington, photograph by Edward Curtis)

Page 69 Top

A Skokomish Indian camp on Hood Canal. (Courtesy of the Washington State Historical Society, Tacoma, Washington, photograph by Edward Curtis)

Page 69 Bottom

Skokomish Indian camp on Skokomish River. (Courtesy of the Washington State Historical Society, Tacoma, Washington, photograph by Edward Curtis)

Page 70 Top

Skokomish Indian baskets. (Courtesy of the Washington
State   Historical   Society,   Tacoma,   Washington,
photograph by Edward Curtis)

Page 70 Bottom

A Skokomish Indian mat shelter. (Courtesy of the
Washington   State   Historical   Society,   Tacoma,
Washington, photograph by Edward Curtis)

Chapter 5

COMMON PLANTS

The wide variety of plants on Hood Canal are the result of numerous habitats existing between saltwater and the high mountains. This wide range of habitats so close together is one of the principal characteristics of Hood Canal.

HABITATS

It may not be evident at first but Hood Canal has five distinct habitats.

The first habitat is marsh areas around river mouths such as at the Skokomish, Hamma Hamma, Duckabush, Dosewallips, and Quilcene Rivers. This habitat consists of grasses, sedges, and other herby vegetation and small willows and alders.

The second habitat goes from sea level to timberline at 2,000--3,000 feet and consists of forests of hemlock, fir and cedar. These forests also contain another habitat made up of small pools of standing water and lots of moss and vegetation.

Above the forest is the semialpine region consisting of small dwarf alpine trees such as alpine hemlock and low growing vegetation.

Above this zone is the true alpine region consisting of alpine tundra and rocky alpine country. The study of these various habitats and their plant life is fascinating.

You may want to bring along *The Audubon Society Field Guide to North American Wildflowers*, Western Region and *The Audubon Society Field Guide to North American Trees*, Western Region. The following descriptions and pictures of some of the plants of Hood Canal will give you an idea of what there is.

TREES

BIGLEAF MAPLE

The Bigleaf Maple grows 30--70' (9--21 m) tall and has a width of 1--2 1/2' (0.3--0.8 m). The leaves are 6--10" (15--25 cm) long and wide, with 5 deep, long-pointed lobes. The bark is brown with furrows making small 4-sided plates. In the spring it has 1/4" (6 mm) yellow flowers in drooping clusters to 6" (15cm). The fruit is a 1--1 1/2" (2.5--4 cm) brown pared "wing" maturing in the autumn.

The Indians made canoe paddles from its wood and maple sugar comes from its sap. The Bigleaf Maples at Hood Canal provide shade in the summer and put on a spectacular display of color when their leaves change to orange and yellow in the fall.

DOUGLAS-FIR

The Douglas-fir is a large tree 80--200' (24--61 m) high with a diameter of 2--5' (0.6--1.5 m) or larger. It has a pointed crown and slightly drooping branches. The evergreen (yellow-green) needles are 3/4--1 1/4" (2--3 cm) long, flattened, mainly rounded at the tip, very short twisted leafstalks, and spreading mainly in 2 rows. The cones are large, 2--3 1/2" (5--9 cm) long, with 3-pointed spreading bracts. The bark is reddish-brown, very thick, and deeply furrowed into broad ridges. The coast Douglas-fir grows well in pure stands in the moist, well-drained soils of the Hood Canal area. It is number one in the United States in total volume of timber, in lumber production, and in production of veneer for plywood. It is one of the tallest trees and is also popular as a Christmas tree. Its foliage provides nutrition for grouse, deer, and elk and its seeds are eaten by birds and mammals.

WESTERN REDCEDAR

The Western Redcedar is a large evergreen which can grow as high as 175' (53 m) or more with a base as wide as 8' (2.4 m) or more. The tree is aromatic and has thin, fibrous, reddish-brown bark. The needles are shiny dark green and form fanlike sprays with 1/2" cones growing upright in clusters near the ends of the twigs. The Western Redcedar resists rot and is used for siding, fenceposts, paneling, boatbuilding, shakes and shingles. The Twana Indians used the giant trunks to carve their canoes from and they split lumber for their plank houses out of the soft durable wood. They also used the bark for rope, roof thatching, mats, baskets and clothing. The giant Western Redcedar stumps located throughout the Hood Canal area are sad reminders of the virgin stands which once grew here.

WESTERN HEMLOCK

The Western Hemlock is a tall slender evergreen which can grow to a height of 150' (46 m) and a diameter of 4' (1.2 m). The shiny dark green needles are short, flexible, flat and rounded at the tip. The needles grow on opposite sides of the twig giving it a flat shape. The branches are horizontal or slightly drooping, especially when the 3/4--1" (2--2.5 cm) cones have formed on the ends of the twigs. The bark is grayish-brown and has deep furrows forming broad, scaly ridges. The Western Hemlock with straight grain and few knots is used for general construction lumber. The poorer quality Western Hemlock is one of the best pulpwoods and provides alpha cellulose for making cellophane, rayon yarns and plastics. Historically, the inner bark was used by the Indians for making bread.

RED ALDER

Red Alder vary in size from a shrub to a tree 40--100' (12--30 m) tall with a diameter of 2 1/2' (0.8 m) or larger. The bark is smooth to slightly scaly and a patchy light gray to whitish color. The leaves are dark green on top and light green underneath with an elliptical shape and saw-toothed edges. The cones are 1/2--1" (1.2--2.5 cm) long and mature in the late summer with small, rounded, flat nutlets having 2 narrow wings.

Red Alder is the most common deciduous or broadleaf tree in the Hood Canal area. It is known as a pioneer species because it quickly takes root in areas where the soil has been disturbed: logging sites, roads and ditches, and along rivers and streams. Red Alder thickets improve the soil and provide cover for the seedlings of the next evergreen forest. The Red Alders disappear as soon as the evergreens overtake them in size because they are intolerant of shade. The Indians have long used Red Alder for smoking fish and firewood.

BERRIES AND OTHER FOREST PLANTS

SALMONBERRY

Salmonberries have bright green leaves and prickly canes which can reach a summer height of 10' (3.0 m). They blossom in the spring with a psychedelic pink flower which is star-shaped. The fruit appears in July and has a mild but slightly tangy flavor. The berries are large and a salmon color on some plants and a dark red-orange on others. The Salmonberry is a common plant in the Hood Canal area and spreads rapidly over any available area making an impenetrable barrier. Their fruit appeals to bears.

DWARF BRAMBLE

The Dwarf Bramble is a common low creeper in the Hood Canal area. It has 4" (10cm) floral stalks having 1 leaf and 1 or 2 white flowers producing a tasty small red raspberry. The white flowers are about 1/2" (1.3 cm) wide with 5 broad petals and numerous stamens. The leaves are 1--2 1/2" (2.5--6.3 cm) long and wide, have toothed edges and are split into 3 lobes. The Dwarf Bramble trails along the ground up to 7' (2.1 m) and is thornless but other species are shrublike, thorny, impenetrable patches producing blackberries and large raspberries.

SALAL

Salal is shrub-like and can grow to a height of 4--48" (10--120 cm). Its spreading or erect hairy stems often grow in large dense patches, and Salal has pale pink, urn-shaped flowers hanging along reddish or salmon racemes in upper axils. The flowers are 3/8" (9 mm) long, and around their opening have 5 pointed lobes. The leaves are 2--4" (5--10 cm) long, ovate, and have numerous small teeth along their edges. Salal produces a dark purple berry 1/4--1/2" (6--13 mm) in diameter and flowers May--July. The Indians used Salal berries to make a thick, sweet syrup and dried the berries and then pounded them into meal which they stored and used in the winter. The settlers also used the berries for making a syrup and also for fresh pies. Today the evergreen leaves are used by the florist trade in floral arrangements.

RED HUCKLEBERRY

The Red Huckleberry is a shrub with somewhat sparse and sharply angled green branches and twigs, red berries, and thin leaves. It can reach a height of 4--12' (1.2--3.6 m). It has bright green bark, greenish to whitish flowers, and bright red, sweet edible berries about 1/4" (6 mm) in diameter. It can be found in shady, humid forests. Deer browse on its leaves and bears like to eat its berries. Rainbow Campground has an abundance of Red Huckleberry.

WILDFLOWERS

YELLOW SKUNK CABBAGE

The Yellow Skunk Cabbage has a spike with minute flowers surrounded by a bright yellow leaf open on one side. The plant grows from a stout stalk and is surrounded by a cluster of shiny green, oval shaped leaves which can grow to 5' (150 cm). The Yellow Skunk Cabbage derives its name from the odor of its sap and flowers. The underground stem is eaten by animals and was baked and used as a winter food by the Indians. Yellow Skunk Cabbage grows in swampy soil and can easily be viewed along the Dosewallips River Road at Brinnon.

TRILLIUM

The Trillium has one white ovate, 3 petal, flower 1 1/2--3" (3.8--7.5 cm) wide with yellow stamens. The flower grows from the center of a whorl of 3 ovate leaves, 2--8" (5--20 cm) long, without stalks at their base. The Trillium is 4--16" (10--40 cm) high. They flower February--June and become pink or reddish with age. The woodland areas of Twanoh State Park are an ideal habitat for Trilliums. The roots for Trilliums were used by Indians and whites for medicines, principally poultices.

PACIFIC DOGWOOD

The Pacific Dogwood is a tree with a thick rounded crown of mostly horizontal branches with clusters of beautiful white flowers. The tree can grow as high as 50' (15 m) and have a 1' (0.3m) diameter. The shiny green leaves are opposite, 2 1/2--4 1/2" (6--11 cm) long, 1 1/4--2 3/4" (3--7 cm) wide, elliptical, have slightly wavy edges, and 5--6 long, curved veins on each side of a midvein. The bark is reddish-brown and thin and its twigs slender. The flowers are 1/4" (6 mm) wide, having greenish-yellow petals close together in a 1" (2.5 cm) wide head, surrounded by 4--7 large, elliptical, starry, white or pinkish, petal-like bracts 1 1/2--2 1/2" (4--6 cm) long, resulting in a large "flower" 4--6" (10--15 cm) wide. For each springtime blossom it produces shiny red elliptical berries maturing in the fall. The Pacific Dogwood blooms in the spring and often again in the fall when its leaves change to orange or red. The Pacific Dogwood is found throughout the Hood Canal area growing in moist soils on the edges of coniferous forests as an understory tree. The brilliant glistening white "flower" blossoms will brighten up any gray Pacific Northwest day. John James Audubon (1780--1851) was so inspired by its beauty he painted it for his now classic work, *Birds of America* and named it after his friend, Thomas Nuttall (1786-1859), respected British-American botanist and ornithologist.

DEER FOOT; VANILLA LEAF

The Deer Foot consists of pairs of low slender stalks, one stalk (a petiole) has at its tip a round leaf blade with a large broad 3-parted leaf and the other stalk ends in a narrow spike of small white flowers. The leaves are leaflets 2--4" (5--10 cm) long, have blunt teeth on their ends, and the central leaflet can have as many as 8 teeth. The flowers a spike 1--2" (2.5--5 cm) long having no sepals or petals but it does have 6--13 white stamens. The outer stamens are swollen near tip. The Deer Foot flowers April--June and reaches a height of 10--20" (25--50 cm). It can be found in the woods of Hood Canal. This unusual 3-parted fan-shaped leaf was a source of amusement for pioneer children. They would make butterflies out of the two biggest broad shaped leaflets and entertain themselves for hours.

PACIFIC RHODODENDRON

The Pacific Rhododendron is an evergreen shrub which can reach a height of 4--10' (1.2--3 m) and sometimes to 20' (6 m). It has large, deep green, leathery leaves and rounded clusters of large, pink, tubular flowers. The pink flower clusters are up to 6" (15 cm) across. It grows well in the forests of the Hood Canal area in acidic soils. You will know why it is the Washington State flower when you see it blooming in May and June.

COMMON WILD FLOWERS OF THE HOOD CANAL AREA

Water Plantain, *(Alisma plantago-aquatica)**
Water Hemlock, *(Cicuta douglasii)**
Cow Parsnip, *(Heracleum lanatum)**
Yellow Skunk Cabbage, *(Lysichitum americanum)**
Long-tailed Wild Ginger, *(Asarum caudatum)**
Orange Agoseris, *(Agoseris aurantiaca)*
Pale Agoseris, *(Agoseris glauca)*
Heartleaf Arnica, *(Arnica cordifolia)*
Engelmann Aster, *(Aster engelmanni)*
Leafy Aster, *(Aster foliaceus)**
Showy Daisy, *(Erigeron speciosus)*
Arrowleaf Groundsel, *(Senecio triangularis)*
Vanilla Leaf, Deer Foot *(Achlys triphylla)*
Heartleaved Bittercress, *(Cardamine cordifolia)*
Comb Draba, *(Draba oligosperma)*
Watercress, *(Nasturtium officinale)*
Wild Candytuft, *(Thlaspi montanum)*
Bluebell/Harebell/Bluebell of Scotland, *(Campanula rotundifolia)*
Twinflower, *(Linnaea borealis)**
Beautiful Sandwort, *(Arenaria capillaris)*
Pacific Dogwood/Mountain Dogwood/Western Flowering Dogwood, *(Cornus nuttallii)*
Cotton Grass, *(Eriophorum polystachion)*
Teasel, *(Dipsacus sylvestris)*
Kinnikkinnick/Bearberry, *(Arctostaphylos uva-ursi)*
White Heather/Mountain Heather, *(Cassiope mertensiana)*
Salal, *(Gualtheria shallon)*
Alpine Laurel, *(Kalmia microphylla)*
Trapper's Tea, *(Ledum glandulosum)*
Pink Mountain Heather, *(Phyllodoce empetriformis)*
White Rhododendron, *(Rhododendron albiflorum)*
Blue-pod Lupine, *(Lupinus polyphyllus)*
White Loco/Silky Loco/Silverleaf Locoweed, *(Oxytropis sericea)*
Showy Loco, *(Oxytropis splendens)*
Yellow Pea/Golden Pea/Buck Bean/False Lupine, *(Thermopsis montana)*
Red Clover, *(Trifolium pratense)*
White Clover, *(Trifolium repens)*

Cow Clover, *(Trifolium wormskjoldii)*
Golden Smoke/Scrambled Eggs, *(Corydalis aurea)*
Northern Gentian, *(Gentiana amarella)*
Explorer's Gentian, *(Gentiana calycosa)*
Fringed Gentian, *(Gentiana detonsa)*
Felwort/Star Swertia, *(Swertia perennis)*
Pacific Waterleaf, *(Hydrophyllum fendleri)*
Tinker's Penny, *(Hypericum anagalloides)*
Blue-eyed Grass, *(Sisyrinchium augustifolium)*
Creeping Charlie/Ground Ivy, *(Glecoma hederacea)*
Field Mint, *(Mentha arvensis)*
Marsh Skullcap, *(Scutellaria galericulata)*
Great Hedge Nettle, *(Stachys cooleyae)**
Common Butterwort, *(Pinguicula vulgaris)**
Nodding Onion, *(Allium cernuum)*
Queen's Cup/Bride's Bonnet, *(Clintonia uniflora)**
Smith's Fairybell, *(Disporum smithii)**
Avalanche Lily/Glacier Lily, *(Erythronium montanum)*
False Lily of the Valley, *(Maianthemum dilatatum)**
False Solomon's Seal, *(Smilacina racemosa)**
Stenanthium, *(Stenanthium occidentale)**
Rosy Twisted-stalk, *(Streptopus roseus)**
Sticky Tofieldia, *(Tofieldia glutinosa)**
Western Wake Robin/Trillium, *(Trillium ovatum)**
Elegant Camas/Alkali Grass, *(Zigadenus elegans)*
Enchanter's Nightshade, *(Circaea alpina)*
Clustered Lady's Slipper, *(Cypripedium fasciculatum)*
Mountain Lady's Slipper, *(Cypripedium montanum)*
Stream Orchid/Chatterbox/Giant Helleborine, *(Epipactis gigantea)*
Western Polemonium, *(Polemonium occidentale)*
Water Smartweed/Water Lady's Thumb, *(Polygonum amphibium)*
Western Bistort/Smokeweed, *(Polygonum bistortoides)**
Spring Beauty, *(Claytonia lanceolata)*
Western Spring Beauty, *(Montia sibirica)*
Miner's Lettuce/Indian Lettuce, *(Montia perfoliata)**
Northern Fairy Candelabra, *(Androsace septentrionalis)**
Few-flowered Shooting Star, *(Dodecatheon pulchellum)*
Western Starflower, *(Trientalis latifolia)*
Little Pipsissewa, *(Chimaphila menziesii)*
Bog Wintergreen, *(Pyrola asarifolia)*
One-sided Wintergreen/Side-Bells, *(Pyrola secunda)*

Meadow Rue, *(Thalictrum occidentale)*
Globeflower, *(Trollius laxus)*
Goatsbeard, *(Aruncus sylvester)**
White Mountain Avens, *(Dryas octopetala)*
Large-leaved Geum, (Geum macrophyllum)
Pacific Silverweed, (Potentilla pacifica)
Dwarf Bramble, *(Rubus lasiococcus)**
Coast Boykinia, *(Boykinia elata)**
Leatherleaf Saxifrage, *(Leptarrhena pyrolifolia)*
Five-point Bishop's Cap, *(Mitella pentandra)*
Fringed Grass of Parnassus, *(Parnassia fimbriata)**
Merten's Saxifrage, *(Saxifraga mertensiana)**
Western Saxifrage, *(Saxifraga occidentalis)*
Alpine Saxifrage, *(Saxifraga tolmiei)*
Violet Suksdorfia, *(Suksdorfia violaceae)*
Fringe Cups, *(Tellima grandiflora)*
False mitrewort, *(Tiarella unifoliata)*
Giant Red Paintbrush, *(Castilleja miniata)*
Seep-spring   Monkeyflower/Common _ Monkey- flower,
(Mimulus guttatus)
Lewis' Monkeyflower, *(Mimulus lewisii)*
Towering Lousewort, *(Pedicularis bracteosa)*
Elephant   Heads/Little   Red   Elephants,   *(Pedicularis*
groenlandica)
Davidson's Penstemon, *(Penstemon davidsonii)*
Cascade Penstemon, *(Penstemon serrulatus)*
Blue Violet, *(Viola adunca)*
Canada Violet, *(Viola canadensis)*
Stream ·Violet/Pioneer Violet/Smooth Yellow Violet,
(Viola glabella)
Redwood Violet/Evergreen Violet/*(Viola sempervirens)**

* Very common

Chapter 6

WILDLIFE

Hood Canal offers a wide range of wildlife for your viewing: land animals, marine mammals, birds, and seashore creatures. If you are quiet and watchful you will be continually surprised and fascinated by what you will see. The following is a sampling of the more common wildlife. You may want to bring along the following Audubon guides: *The Audubon Society Field Guide to North American Mammals*, *The Audubon Society Field Guide to North American Fishes, Whales, and Dolphins*, *The Audubon Society Field Guide to North American Seashells*, *The Audubon Society Field Guide to North American Seashore Creatures*, and *The Audubon Society Field Guide to North American Birds*, Western Region.

LAND ANIMALS

ROOSEVELT ELK

The Elk is a large deer with slender legs and a thick neck. The Roosevelt Elk has a shoulder height of 4 1/2--5' (137--150 cm) and a length of 6 3/4--9 3/4' (2,032--2,972 mm). The male weighs 600--1,089 lb. (270--495 kg)

and the female weighs 450--650 lb. (203--293 kg). The
Elk is brown or tan above with darker underparts and
the males have a dark brown mane on their throats.
The Elks most distinctive color feature is its yellowish-
brown rump patch. There are six subspecies of Elk and
two are found in Washington--the Roosevelt Elk and the
Rocky Mountain Elk or Yellowstone Elk. The Roosevelt
Elk are native to the Olympic Peninsula and Hood Canal
area and the Rocky Mountain Elk were imported from
Montana. The Roosevelt Elk is about 5% larger than the
Rocky Mountain Elk and slightly lighter in color.

Your best chance to see Roosevelt Elk is in the
early spring when the herds on the Dosewallips and
Duckabush Rivers come down to the river mouths to
feed on the fresh spring grasses and sedges. The illustration of Roosevelt Elk by Richard Amundsen illustrates the sight you would have in store for yourself.
The proud bull Elk in the foreground is shown with his
harem of three cows although bulls can assemble harems
of up to 60 cows. The bull Elk in the drawing has a
full set of antlers with 6 points or "tines" on each side
and a main 5' beam and is known as a "Royal" head.
Antler descriptions go back to medieval times and are
still used today. The first tine is called the "brow" tine
or eye guard; the second the "bay" or "bez" tine; the
third tine is called the "trez" tine; the fourth point on
the outermost curve of the antler is called the "royal"
or "dagger" point; and the remaining points forking off
the end of the main beam are called "sur-royals".

Elk were once prevalent in most of southern Canada
and the United States but loss of habitat due to farming and the encroachment of civilization drastically reduced their numbers. Today the herds of the Duckabush
and Dosewallips Rivers of Hood Canal are facing the
same pressures from the loss of habitat due to logging
and the encroachment of civilization.

BEAVER

The Beaver is a large dark brown rodent 35 1/2--46" (900--1170 mm) long and 11 3/4--17 3/8" (300--440 mm) tall. They usually weigh 45--60 lbs (20.3--27 kg) but can weigh up to 109 lbs. (49.5 kg). They have small eyes and ears, a large black, horizontally flattened, paddle-shaped, scaly tail, and large black, webbed hindfeet. The Beaver is known for his dams and lodges of woven sticks and branches. He also dredges canals where he actually changes the water levels to float his construction material to the Beaver pond. The drawing by Richard Amundsen captures the uniqueness of the Beaver. The pictures below are of a Beaver lodge, dam, and canal, in the Lake Cushman area, which is an ideal habitat for the Beaver with its many streams, marshes, lakes, and ponds. The pictures were taken in the summer and the water level of the Beaver pond was very low. You can see the underwater entrance to the lodge.

BLACK-TAILED DEER

The Black-tailed Deer is 3--3 1/2' (90--105 cm) high at the shoulders and 3 3/4--6 1/2' (116--199 cm) long. The male weighs 110--475 lb. (50--215 kg) and the female weighs 70--160 lb. (31.5--72 kg). Its ears are 4 3/4--6" long (12--15 cm) and its antlers fork into equal branches. The Black-tailed Deer derived its name from its tail which is blackish or brown above and white underneath. In summer the Black-tailed Deer is reddish-brown above and in winter grayish above. The throat patch, rump patch and inside of legs and ears are white, and the lower parts cream to tan.

Your best chance to see deer is in the spring when the doe with her newborn fawn or fawns come down to the lowlands to nibble on new grass. The picture of a Black-tailed Deer was taken only a few feet from the highway on the Toandos Peninsula going to Coyle. As the picture shows a common trait of the Black-tailed Deer are its large ears. These ears move constantly and independently of each other and account for the common name--Mule Deer, of which the Black-tailed Deer is a major subspecies. Deer are common in the Hood Canal area and when you are driving always respect deer crossing signs and reduce your speed.

In May and June the deer migrate to the mountain meadows where they will spend the summer eating mainly herbaceous plants but also blackberry, salal and thimbleberry. As fall approaches and the frost starts to limit their food supply they start moving down to the forests where they will spend the winter browsing on Douglas fir and cedar twigs, and foraging among the leaves and shrubs. If the winter snow is severe they will be forced down to the beaches to look for dried grass to eat or even seaweed under extreme circumstances.

WESTERN GRAY SQUIRREL

The Western Gray Squirrel is 17 1/2--23 1/4" (445--593 mm) long. As the picture shows the Western Gray Squirrel has numerous white-tipped hairs and a long bushy tail with bands of gray, white, and black. It is interesting to note the uses of its tail: an umbrella for the rain, a rudder when it swims, providing lift when it jumps from branch to branch, and if it falls a means of slowing descent, and a blanket in the winter. Chewed fir cones scattered on the ground are a sure sign of its presence. The Western Gray Squirrel is a common sight in the woodlands of Hood Canal.

MARINE MAMMALS

HARBOR SEAL

The Harbor Seal or "Hair Seal" is 4--5' 7" (120--170 cm) long and weighs up to 300 lb. (136 kg). It is yellowish-gray or brownish with dark spots above. It is a true seal, meaning it has no ears and cannot rotate its flippers forward making it clumsy on land. It eats mainly fish such as herring, rockfish, flounder, cod, salmon, and also clams, crab, octopus and shrimp. It does spend sometime on land resting and having its young. Harbor Seals anger commercial fishermen because they are very good at stealing salmon from their nets or trolling lines, and for many years there was a bounty on Harbor Seals.

Harbor Seals are very common on Hood Canal. You will usually see the Harbor Seal by itself or with another. The Harbor Seal will poke its head slightly out of the water to look at you and when seen quickly submerges. It may repeat the above numerous times at varying distances from your boat until its curiosity is satisfied and it swims on. Harbor seals have also become an aggravation on Hood Canal because their large numbers are causing a pollution which has resulted in the closing of shellfish harvesting around Dosewallips State Park.

RIVER OTTER

The River Otter has an elongated body 35--51 5/8" (889--1,313 mm) long, 11 3/4--20" (300--507 mm) thick, and weighs 11--30 lb. (5--13.6 kg). Its fur is dark brown but looks black when wet and its throat is silver-gray with long whitish whiskers. Its tail is thick at the base gradually tapering to a point and makes up one third of its body length. The River Otter is at home on land and in both fresh and saltwater. The River Otter is a powerful, graceful swimmer and lives mainly on fish but also eats small land animals such as mice. It lives in a small den dug into the side of a riverbank which has an underwater and above ground entrance.

The illustration by Richard Amundsen of two River Otters was inspired by photographs I took of River Otters around the mouth of Dewatto Bay on the east side of Hood Canal.

The River Otters highly prized pelts nearly led to its extinction and more recently water and air pollution, including mercury fallout, have threatened its survival. Studies indicate, however, some River Otters are developing a tolerance to toxic substances, and their numbers may be slowly increasing on Hood Canal.

FISH AND SHELLFISH

CHUM SALMON

The most common salmon on Hood Canal is the Chum (Dog) Salmon. The Chum Salmon is around 33" (84 cm) long. Its fins are usually dark-tipped and the dorsal can be pale at the edges. The spawning adults have reddish bars, large pale blotches on their sides, and the tips of the pelvic and anal fins will be white. They spend four years in the saltwater before returning to their home streams to spawn. The young will stay in the streams for only two days before migrating to the ocean. You will be able to observe them spawning in the small streams of Twanoh State Park or Belfair State Park in the fall around October. Seeing them heading up these small shallow streams is a sight you won't want to miss.

CUTTHROAT TROUT

Cutthroat Trout, or "native trout", vary in color and size. The most common size is around 15" (38 cm) long and in coloration its back is dark olive and its sides are variable: silvery, olive, reddish to yellow-orange; and its belly is whitish. It can be identified by dark spots on its back, sides, and median fins and by a bright red to red-orange slash mark on each side of the throat. Its habitat is inshore marine and estuarine waters, lakes, and coastal, inland and alpine streams.

COMMON PACIFIC LITTLENECK

The Common Pacific Littleneck is 1 1/2--2 3/8" (3.8--6 cm) long with a broad and ovately oblong shape. Its exterior is yellowish-white or brownish and sometimes it has large brownish splotches or zigzag markings and spots. It has many fine crowded riblets and its interior is white. It is found a few inches deep in gravelly sand and mud in the lower half of the intertidal zone in bays. Some Hood Canal public beaches have an abundance of these clams as the picture shows.

PACIFIC OYSTER

The Pacific Oyster is 2--12" (5.1--30.5 cm) long with a grayish-white exterior and a white interior. It has a somewhat long egg shape narrowing at its upper end and has noticeable ridges and grooves which are its growth lines. The Pacific Oyster is common throughout all of Hood Canal being found on rocks, soft mud, firm sand and gravel above or below the tide line. The Pacific Oyster is also called the Japanese Oyster or Miyagi Oyster.

The illustration of the Pacific Oyster and the Glaucous-winged Gull by Richard Amundsen is unique.

GLAUCOUS-WINGED GULL

The Glaucous-winged Gull is a large white gull 24--27" (61--69 cm) long with a pearly gray mantle and wings. It has a red spot on its bill which becomes black in winter. Its voice is a series of rough sounding similar notes of the same pitch and when alarmed a series of dull ga-ga-ga notes. It feeds mainly along the shore line eating dead seabirds, clams, mussels, starfish, etc. but occasionally feeds over water eating dead or dying fish. When living close to people it is a garbage scavenger. Its range is from the Aleutians and Bering Sea south to Oregon.

SEASHORE CREATURE

SPOT SHRIMP

The Spot Shrimp, which Hood Canal is famous for, may reach 10" long and has distinctive white spots on its tail. It is pink with 10 legs, long antenna, and prominent white markings along its side. It is found in 30 to 300' of water.

BIRDS

BRANT
"BLACK BRANT"

The "Black Brant" is a Mallard-sized goose 23--26" (58--66 cm) long. Their head, neck, chest, back, wings, and tail are black and contrast greatly with their snow white lower belly, flanks, and undertail--especially in flight. On water it seems entirely black except for a white collar. It breeds on the coastal tundra of Alaska and northwestern Canada and winters on the Pacific Coast with large numbers on Puget Sound and Hood Canals bays and estuaries. It is a saltwater bird feeding on eelgrass and sea lettuce and seldom flies inland to freshwater.

The "Black Brant" was hunted by the early pioneers of Hood Canal and was important to their well-being as the following quote from *With Pride In Heritage* (Port Townsend: Jefferson County Historical Society, 1966, 292) shows:

> It must be remembered too that nothing was lost of the migratory birds. There was a delicious dinner in store for those who had taken the time to make a short trip and there were feathered pillows and a feather tick for sleeping comfort as well. History may well have taught us a lesson in conservation that has long since been ignored and forgotten. Not so with the pioneers.

The "Black Brant" is still hunted but its greatest danger is loss of winter habitats to encroaching civilization.

The illustration by Richard Amundsen of "Black Brant" on Hood Canal captures the essence of this unique black-and-white bird and if you're fortunate enough to see a formation of "Black Brant" it will be more memorable than seeing a black Stealth bomber in flight.

GREAT BLUE HERON

The Great Blue Heron is 42--52" (107--132 cm) long and 48" (122 cm) tall. Its back and wings are blue-gray; its underparts are whitish with black streaks on the belly; and its head is white with a black stripe terminating in black plumes behind the eyes. Its habitat is wetlands with tall trees and grasses providing protection for the heronry. Hood Canal is an ideal habitat. The Great Blue Heron is found throughout North America except in the colder northern areas and as far south as South America. It nests in stick nests in colonies often with numerous nests in the same tree.

The picture shows a Great Blue Heron a short distance from U.S. Highway 101 at Brinnon silently fishing.

TRUMPETER SWAN

The Trumpeter Swan is one of North America's largest birds measuring 60--72" (150--180 cm) and weighing as much as 28 lb. (over 12.5 kg). It is snow white with a large black bill. As a boy I often went to the park with my grandmother and admired the Mute Swan which is similar to the Trumpeter Swan. The Mute Swan, however, is a tame pond bird, is smaller with a black knob at the base of its orange bill, and holds its neck in a graceful curve with its bill pointing downward. The native Trumpeter Swan swims with its neck straight and bill held horizontal. The Trumpeter Swan has a booming, horn-like ko-hoh call. Their habitat is marshes, lakes, or rivers with thick vegetation. Its huge nest, built on a bullrush-covered island or beaver lodge, will contain 4--6 whitish eggs. The Trumpeter Swan does not breed until it is four years of age, making their reproduction slow. The Trumpeter Swan spends the winter in southeastern Alaska, western British Columbia and open waters of the United States. They breed in southern Alaska, northern British Columbia, western Alberta, Oregon, Idaho, Montana, and Wyoming.

In the 1930's they were close to extinction due to hunting and loss of habitat, but conservation measures, and reintroduction into former marshy areas has brought their number to over 3,000.

The illustration of Trumpeter Swans by Richard Amundsen was based on photographs I took of a flock which stopped over on their way north. They could be seen daily for a couple weeks resting on the marshy area at the mouth of the Dosewallips River on Hood Canal. As the drawing illustrates they are a very inspiring sight.

CANADA GOOSE

The Canada Goose is 22--45" (56--92. cm) long and can weigh up to 13 lb. (5.9 kg). It has a long black neck, head, and bill and white cheek patches. Its lower belly and small feathers covering the bases of the larger feathers on the wings and tail are white and its tail and rump are black. They are called "Canadian Honkers" by many people because of the noise they make while flying in formation or when one becomes separated from the flock. Its habitat varies from marsh and lake areas to prairie sloughs. It usually nests in marshy areas, and the nest will have 4--8 large white eggs. It breeds in the spring across northern North America from Alaska to Labrador, south to the mid-Atlantic states, Kansas and California. During the fall they leave their breeding grounds and migrate to the southwestern or Pacific coastal states for the winter. Before the Canada Geese migrate they molt all their flying feathers. They are unable to fly for a couple weeks. When their molting is complete they fly to their winter grounds. The migratory route and location of the winter home is taught to the young geese in one flight.

The picture was taken at the Skokomish Tidelands and shows Canada Geese resting along the shoreline.

RUFFED GROUSE

The Ruffed Grouse or "Native Pheasant" is a chicken-sized bird 16--19" (41--48 cm). The Ruffed Grouse is mottled, reddish-brown in appearance and has a fan-shaped tail with a black band at its end. The Ruffed Grouse is also characterized by a slight crest, buff streaks above and brown-reddish cross-barring below. The male has a ruff of erectile black feathers on either side of the neck. The female is plainer and has a smaller tail and ruff. Their habitat is along the edges of coniferous forest and deciduous woodlands. Their range is from the northern limit of the coniferous forest in North America south to the limit of the coniferous forest growth. The picture was taken on the edge of the coniferous forest growth near the Hamma Hamma River road on Hood Canal. The female was being defiant as can be seen from her raised crest and spreading tail because her chicks were only a short distance away.

The Ruffed Grouse is a native game bird of Washington and is underutilized by hunters and could be hunted at a greater rate. Interestingly, a greater harvest rate would reduce its overwinter mortality. The Ruffed Grouse could be hunted with a dog like pheasant. Most hunters have not hunted the Ruffed Grouse in this manner.

HARLEQUIN DUCK

The Harlequin Duck measures 14 1/2--21" (37--53 cm). It was named Harlequin because the slate blue breeding male with bright chestnut flanks has markings like a clown--bold white markings outlined in black, especially noticeable on head and wings. The female and non-breeding male are dark with two or three small white patches on their heads and the male has some white on his wings. As the picture of the breeding male Harlequin (clown) Duck shows its habitat during the nesting season around April is rushing water around boulders in mountain streams--the Dosewallips River on Hood Canal. The male will return the end of June or later to his habitat of rocky headlands and islets subject to strong currents in the Georgia Strait and Puget Sound areas of British Columbia and Washington. Besides the mountainous Pacific North America region its range is Baffin Island, Greenland, Iceland; Alaska to California and Wyoming; and Eastern Siberia.

As you explore Hood Canal the sighting of a Harlequin Duck will make you as happy as any clown can--I guarantee it.

COMMON BIRDS OF HOOD CANAL

Spotted Sandpiper, *(Actitis macularia)*
Osprey, *(Pandion haliaetus)*
Bald Eagle, *(Haliaeetus leucocephalus)*
Rough-winged Swallow, *(Stelgidopteryx ruficollis)**
Tree Swallow, *(Iridoprocne bicolor)*
Dipper, *(Cinclus mexicanus)**
Belted Kingfisher, *(Megaceryle alcyon)*
Lapland Longspur, *(Calcarius lapponicus)*
Red-tailed Hawk, *(Buteo jamaicensis)*
American Kestrel/"Sparrow Hawk", *(Falco sparverius)*
Western Meadowlark, *(Sturnella neglecta)*
Savannah Sparrow, *(Passerculus sandwichensis)*
Horned Lark, *(Eremophila alpestris)*
Gray-crowned Rosy Finch, *(Leucosticte tephrocotis)*
Water Pipit, *(Anthus spinoletta)*
Tree Sparrow, *(Spizella arborea)*
American Robin/"Robin",*(Turdus migratorius)*
Starling, *(Sturnus vulgaris)*
Rufous-sided Towhee, *(Pipilo erythrophthalmus)*
Ruffed Grouse, *(Bonasa umbellus)**
Great Horned Owl, *(Bubo virginianus)**
Long-eared Owl, *(Asio otus)*
Cooper's Hawk, *(Accipiter cooperii)*
Downy Woodpecker, *(Picoides pubescens)**
Common Flicker/"Red-shafted Flicker", *(Colaptes auratus)*
"Red-breasted Sapsucker", *(Sphyrapicus varius)*
Wilson's Warbler, *(Wilsonia pusilla)*
Yellow Warbler, *(Dendroica petechia)**
MacGillivray's Warbler, *(Oporornis tolmiei)*
Black-headed Grosbeak, *(Pheucticus melanocephalus)*
Gray Catbird/"Catbird", *(Dumetella carolinensis)*
Orange-crowned Warbler, *(Vermivora celata)*
Warbling Vireo, *(Vireo gilvus)*
Red-eyed Vireo, *(Vireo olivaceus)**
Solitary Vireo, *(Vireo solitarius)*
Bewick's Wren, *(Thryomanes bewickii)*
Housewren *(Troglodytes aedon)*
Swainson's Thrush, *(Catharus ustulatus)*
Brown-headed Cowbird, *(Molothrus ater)*
Fox Sparrow, *(Passerella iliaca)*

Song Sparrow, *(Melospiza melodia)*
Common Raven, *(Corvus corax)**
Blue Grouse, *(Dendragapus obscurus)**
Pygmy Owl, *(Glaucidium gnoma)*
Spotted Owl, *(Strix occidentalis)*
Thayer's Gull, *(Larus thayeri)*
Herring Gull, *(Larus argentatus)*
Glaucous-winged Gull, *(Larus glaucescens)**
Western Gull, *(Larus occidentalis)*
Mew Gull, *(Larus canus)*
Marbled Murrelet, *(Brachyramphus marmoratus)*
Black Scoter/"Common Scoter", *(Melanitta nigra)*
Dunlin, *(Calidris alpina)*
Sharp-tailed Sandpiper, *(Calidris acuminata)*
Gyrfalcon, *(Falco rusticolus)*
Fork-tailed Storm-Petrel/"Fork-tailed Petrel", (Oceanodroma furcata)
Pelagic Cormorant, *(Phalacrocorax pelagicus)*
Rhinoceros Auklet, *(Cerorhinca monocerata)*
Rock Sandpiper, *(Calidris ptilocnemis)*
Black Turnstone, *(Arenaria melanocephala)**
Surfbird, *(Aphriza virgata)*
Tufted Duck, *(Aythya fuligula)*
Greater Scaup, *(Aythya marila)*
American Bittern, *(Botaurus lentiginosus)*
Great Blue Heron, *(Ardea herodias)*
Canvasback, *(Aythya valisineria)*
Northern Shoveler/"Shoveler", *(Anas clypeata)*
Mallard, *(Anas platyrhynchos)*
American Coot, *(Fulica americana)*
European Wigeon, *(Anas penelope)*
American Wigeon, *(Anas americana)*
Green-winged Teal, *(Anas crecca)*
Pintail, *(Anas acuta)*
Trumpeter Swan, *(Olor buccinator)*
Canada Goose, *(Branta canadensis)*
Common Snipe/"Wilson's Snipe", *(Capella gallinago)*
Short-eared Owl, *(Asio flammeus)*
Marsh Hawk, (Circus cyaneus)
Common Yellowthroat/"Yellowthroat", *(Geothlypis trichas)*
Long-billed Marsh Wren, *(Cistothorus palustris)*
Red-winged Blackbird, *(Agelaius phoeniceus)*

Common Merganser, *(Mergus merganser)*
Hooded Merganser, *(Lophodytes cucullatus)*
Bufflehead, *(Bucephala albeola)*
Barrow's Goldeneye, *(Bucephala islandica)*
Common Goldeneye, *(Bucephala clangula)*
Wood Duck, *(Aix sponsa)*
Harlequin Duck, *(Histronicus histrionicus)*
Common Loon, *(Gavia immer)*
Western Grebe, *(Aechmophorus occidentalis)*
Red-necked Grebe, *(Podiceps grisegena)*
Pied-billed Grebe, *(Podilymbus podiceps)*
Horned Grebe, *(Podiceps auritus)*
Killdeer, *(Charadrius vociferus)*
Sharp-shinned Hawk, *(Accipiter striatus)*
Goshawk, *(Accipiter gentilis)*
Merlin/"Pigeon Hawk", *(Falco columbarius)*
Violet-green Swallow, *(Tachycineta thalassina)*
Vaux's Swift, *(Chaetura vauxi)**
Hairy Woodpecker, *(Picoides villosus)**
Northern Three-toed Woodpecker, *(Picoides tridactylus)**
Red-breasted Nuthatch, *(Sitta canadensis)*
Brown Creeper, *(Certhia familiaris)*
Rufous Hummingbird, *(Selasphorus rufus)*
Yellow-rumped Warbler, *(Dendroica coronata)*

* Year-round resident

Chapter 7

SIGHTS ALONG THE WAY

The sights along the way as you explore Hood Canal are varied and numerous: mountains, rivers, waterfalls, oyster farms, clear-cutting, purseseiners, fish hatcheries, Mt. Walker, historic structures, Christmas tree farms, geology, Whitney Gardens and Nursery, salmon stands, seafood stores, and smokehouses, fire cracker stands, shrimp fishermen, smelt fishermen, ancient forests, Wilcox Mansion, Camp Parsons, scuba divers, Trident submarines, logging trucks, logging trestle ruins, Point Whitney Shellfish Laboratory, Dalby Waterwheel, Lake Cushman Dam and Power Plant, Hood Canal Floating Bridge.

PURSESEINERS

Purseseiners are the most distinguished boats of the fishing fleet. Purseseiners can be identified by their size, 50-60 feet, wide beam, large afterdeck, high mast and boom and a large circular power winch or block attached to the end of the boom. When the purseseiner is not fishing its large net with its floats will be piled on the afterdeck and a 19 foot seine skiff will be stored upside down on top of the net. Many purseseiners were series built and are almost identical in appearance.

The fishing areas open to purseseining are large and a purseseiner will travel many miles during the season searching for fish. When fishing starts the seine skiff will be put in the water and the end of the net attached to it. The seine skiff then sets the net out in a circle creating a fence around the fish. There is a drawstring or purseline around the bottom of the net and it is pulled or pursed drawing the bottom of the net together making a purse shape out of it. One end of the net is then hoisted aboard through the large circular power winch attached to the boom. As the net is taken aboard it is piled on the afterdeck and the net left in the water becomes smaller and smaller and closer to the surface until the fish are alongside and can be scooped out. Sometimes if the fish are not in a school the net will be set in a hook shape between the boat and the seine skiff or attached to a tree on shore. The current will then carry the fish into the net and after awhile it will be pursed. Purseseining is the most efficient way of catching salmon, and also the least discriminating. A set may result in nothing, tons of jellyfish, or thousands of salmon. When fishing is good the net is set again and again until the purseseiners iced hold is full. The fish will then be loaded onto a cannery tender to be taken to the cannery or taken to the cannery by the purseseiner, where they will be cleaned and canned. Because salmon caught by purseseining sustain the most damage they are all canned.

RIVERS

The Dosewallips River as of now is still wild and un-tamed as this picture shows.

The Dosewallips, Duckabush, Hamma Hamma, Quilcene and Skokomish Rivers make rapid descents through a series of raging rapids and pools before emp-tying into Hood Canal.

The precipitous Olympic Mountains closeness to Hood Canal are responsible for these rivers dropping so quickly to sea level at Hood Canal and the high annual rainfall and snowfall keeps them raging.

OYSTER FARMS

Along the shore of Dabob Bay lives an oyster farmer named Dick Steele whose father was a pioneer in the oyster industry--E.N. Steele. Pacific Oysters are not native to Washington waters and E.N. Steele was the first oyster farmer to import a large cargo of oyster spat or seed called Ostrea Gigas, now known as the Pacific Oyster, from Japan in 1924. He also founded the Pacific Coast Oyster Growers Association in 1930 which was responsible for importing quality seed from Japan every year assuring the survival and expansion of the Washington oyster industry. With the war the supply of seed was cutoff but it was discovered these oysters reproduced naturally in Quilcene and Dabob Bay. We are no longer dependent on seed from Japan and Quilcene and Dabob Bay now grow quality seed which is sold to oyster growers throughout the world.

FISH HATCHERIES

The state, Indians and federal government all operate fish hatcheries on Hood Canal to preserve and enhance the salmon runs. It is an interesting sight to watch the salmon returning in the fall to the hatcheries (and the fisherman in front of the Hoodsport hatchery) and see how man can successfully intervene in the natural spawning process by: removing the salmon eggs to be spawned in the hatcheries, hatching them in troughs or trays in the hatchery buildings and rearing them to migratory size in the hatchery raceways or ponds and releasing the young salmon into the streams for downstream migration to the ocean.

MOUNTAINS

No matter where you are on Hood Canal you will have an Olympian view of the mountains--Olympian defined as: "befitting or characteristic of Olympus or the Olympian Gods, as in power or dignity; Godlike; awe-inspiring." Hence the name Olympic Mountains.

Sawtooth Ridge, Olympic Mountains

Sawtooth Ridge, Olympic Mountains

Sawtooth Ridge, Olympic Mountains

Sawtooth Ridge, Olympic Mountains

Sawtooth Ridge, Olympic Mountains

Mt. Ellinor and Mt. Washington, Olympic Mountains

Mt. Constance, Olympic Mountains

WATERFALLS

Rush hour on Hood Canal is quite enjoyable as you enjoy the sights and sounds of Hood Canals waterfalls. I have included a picture of Lilliwaup Falls by world famous Asahel Curtis even though it is now closed to the public due to private ownership. Lilliwaup Falls still lives on in the memories of many Hood Canal pioneers who often came from miles around and even from across the canal by rowboats to picnic at the base of this beautiful waterfall. The other falls are still accessible, even though one is on private property. Hood Canal's waterfalls are most magnificent during the spring runoff.

Dosewallips Falls--approximately 13.5 miles from Brinnon on Dosewallips Road and FS Rd 2610.

Rocky Brook Falls--3.0 miles northwest of Brinnon on Dosewallips Road.

Susan's Falls--Lk Cushman Rd to FS Rd 24. Turn right, drive 1.6 mi. Turn left onto FS Rd 2419. Go 6.4 mi.

Lilliwaup Falls. (Courtesy of the Washington State Historical Society, Tacoma, Washington, photo no. 5789)

MT. WALKER

North of Brinnon on U.S. Highway 101 a sign points to Mt. Walker. A two lane gravel road winds up Mt. Walker through beautiful forest land and understory of rhododendron and salal. As you drive higher and higher your views will be impressive but nothing compared to what they will be at the top. To the east you will see Hood Canal and Puget Sound, to the north the Strait of Juan de Fuca and San Juan Islands and Canada, to the west and south the beautiful Olympic Mountains, and if its a really clear day to the east you will be able to see the Space Needle, Kingdome and Seattle. If you venture up this road in the spring or fall snow can make Mt. Walker a winter wonderland. The road is closed in the winter due to it not being plowed for snow.

HAMMA HAMMA GUARD STATION

You reach the historic Hamma Hamma Guard Station by driving six miles up the Hamma Hamma River Road (Forest Service Road #25) from U.S. Highway 101 and right before the Hamma Hamma Campground turning right onto a one lane road and driving a short ways to the guard station. Land for the site was set aside in 1907. The original forest service guard station was built in 1913 and the present structure was built in the 1930's by President Roosevelt's Civilian Conservation Corps (CCC), a program during the depression to get unemployed youth back to work through the building of trails and structures in our national forests and parks. The guard station is a good example of the style of architecture and design used for national park and forest service buildings during the 1930's and has been declared a National Register-eligible structure.

INTERROREM GUARD STATION

The Interrorem Guard Station is located 4 miles up the Duckabush River Road from U.S. Highway 101. You won't want to miss this historic building which was built in 1906 and was the first administrative site on the Olympic National Forest.

SCUBA DIVERS

Scuba divers are a common site along Hood Canal. Hood Canal's clear water and abundant sea life make Hood Canal a popular diving area for scuba divers.

TRIDENT SUBMARINE

And lo! close under our lee, not forty fathoms off, a gigantic Sperm Whale lay rolling in the water like the capsized hull of a frigate, his broad, glossy back, of an Ethiopian hue, glistening in the sun's rays like a mirror. But lazily undulating in the trough of the sea, and ever and anon tranquilly spouting his vapory jet, the whale looked like a portly burgher smoking his pipe of a warm afternoon. But that pipe, poor whale, was thy last. As if struck by some enchanter's wand, the sleepy ship and every sleeper in it all at once started into wakefulness; and more than a score of voices from all parts of the vessel, simultaneously with the three notes from aloft, shouted forth the accustomed cry, as the great fish slowly and regularly spouted the sparkling brine into the air.

The similarities in the above quote from Herman Melvilles *Moby - Dick* to the picture below are interesting, but what you are looking at is a 560' nuclear powered Trident submarine blowing its air tanks and diving. Don't be surprised if you see a Trident sub as you explore Hood Canal.

LOGGING TRUCKS

Hood Canal is logging country--Olympic National Forest, Tahuya State Forest and private forestland and sooner or later you will see these big rigs with their valueable load of logs heading for market.

CLEAR-CUTTING

Clear-cutting is when all the trees in a certain area are cut down. Recent areas of clear-cutting are easy to spot and past areas of clear-cutting are a lighter shade of green than the forests around them. You will notice many areas of clear-cutting on Hood Canal.

Hood Canal has known numerous examples of destructive clear-cutting. Some areas are so bad it is impossible for the coniferous forest to re-establish itself.

Responsible foresters are clear-cutting so that the forest will replenish itself and can be harvested as a continuing crop. Responsible clear-cutting means: The area of clear-cutting is small, the slash is removed by burning, and the area is replanted with seedlings to yield a harvestable forest in the future.

LOGGING TRESTLE RUINS

When I was a boy our family used to spend our summer vacation on Hood Canal. A memory I will never forget is driving high in the mountains with my dad on old roads and seeing old logging trestle ruins. Some of the old roads around Hood Canal are former railroad grades--you can tell them from forest service or logging roads because their grades are moderate. If you follow these roads and look carefully in the ravines you can still find old logging trestle ruins.

POINT WHITNEY SHELLFISH LABORATORY

North of Brinnon on U.S. Highway 101 you will see a sign pointing right to the Point Whitney Shellfish Laboratory. It's only a short drive to the lab which is on the shore of Dabob Bay on Hood Canal. The lab was established by the Washington State Department of Fisheries to do shellfish research. Currently the lab is doing research on a large clam called a Geoduck and operating a hatchery for growing Geoducks for planting in beds on Hood Canal and Puget Sound. When the Geoducks grow to maturity they will be commercially harvested for human consumption.

The lab is closed to the public but a nearby interpretive center has display cases, signs, and scale model displays which explain the hatchery operation and the shellfish found on Hood Canal.

DALBY WATERWHEEL

The Dalby Waterwheel was built in 1926 to generate power. Located near the Alderbrook Resort. Be sure to bring your camera.

HOOD CANAL FLOATING BRIDGE

The Hood Canal Floating Bridge is the worlds largest floating bridge over intertidal waters. Prior to the Hood Canal Floating Bridge people either drove around Hood Canal or took the ferry across from Lofall to South Point to reach the Olympic Peninsula. Built in 1961 the Hood Canal Floating Bridge is 7,860 feet long, is made up of 29 floating pontoons, and has a draw span which opens allowing the passage of submarines and ships. The bridge is held in place against strong currents, waves and winds by 94,840 linear feet of cable secured to 42 anchors. The bridge has served its purpose well except in 1979 when due to a severe storm from the south 4,053 feet of the bridge sank. Ferry service was once again resumed. By 1982 the bridge had been rebuilt and reopened. Occasionally during high winds and waves the bridge is closed and the center draw span opened to relieve pressure on the bridge. This bridge is truly one of the worlds marvels of engineering.

CAMP PARSONS

The Boy Scouts of America was started in 1910 and nine years later Camp Parsons held its first summer camp. The purpose of the camp is shown by the following quote from Boy Scout literature:

> Camping is the great outdoor adventure of Scouting. As a Scout becomes at home in the outdoors, he unconsciously absorbs some of the greatness of nature itself-the stillness of the forest-the merriment of the mountain stream-the breath of the ocean-the freedom of the sky-the clearness of the wind-the beauty of the sunset. In working with nature to help provide his food and comfort, he learns some of the skills, resourcefulness, and self-reliance of the pioneer. The woods, streams, the trails, and the wild creatures that inhabit them become his friends and the outdoors a lifelong source of recreation.

CHRISTMAS TREE FARMS

Not far from the eastern shore of Hood Canal are thousands and thousands of Christmas trees being grown on Christmas tree farms. As early as November some of these trees will be cut and shipped to all parts of the United States and even the world.

GEOLOGY

15,000 years ago Hood Canal was covered by a great glacier nearly a mile high which moved down from Canada. Its movement scoured out Hood Canal over a period of 1.5 million years. This glacier carried down huge granite boulders called erratics from Canada. As the weather warmed the glacier melted forming Lake Hood later to become Hood Canal, and left the huge light gray granite boulders behind, which can still be seen throughout the Hood Canal area.

WHITNEY GARDENS AND NURSERY

Whitney Gardens and Nursery is located at Brinnon on Hood Canal. The nursery was started by the Whitney's in 1955 as a hobby and today is owned by George and Anne Sather who continue the tradition of making the garden nursery ever more beautiful. The garden is open to the public for tours and features over 3,000 rhododendrons, azaleas, and related plants. The rhododendron species range in geographical distribution from Asia, Europe, Australia, New Zealand and the eastern and western United States. The garden also has large trees such as oaks, maples, magnolias, beechs, plums, katsuras, sourwoods and liquid ambers interspersed with deciduous shrubs and companion plants. You won't want to miss the peak of the blooming season which occurs around Mothers' Day.

SALMON STANDS, SEAFOOD STORES

Eastern Washington is famous for its fresh fruit stands and Hood Canal is famous for its fresh salmon stands--you can't buy salmon any fresher. You may also purchase a variety of seafood from Hood Canal's year-round seafood stores--oysters, clams, Hood Canal Spot Shrimp, etc.

FIREWORKS STANDS

Around the fourth of July numerous fireworks stands open on the Skokomish Indian Reservation. As the lettering on the side of the stand says "bottle rockets, firecrackers, and much more!!

SHRIMP FISHERMEN

For a brief time in May or June Hood Canal becomes as crowded and congested as a Southern
California beach town when the temperature goes over
100 degrees. The reason is the famous Hood Canal Spot
Shrimp which is claimed to be the tastiest and biggest
of Washington's seven species of shrimp due to the
clean water and excellent food supply of Hood Canal.
Hood Canal will be full of boats setting and tending
their shrimp traps. The picture shows a shrimp trap
containing 10 pounds, the maximum allowable catch, of
the famous Hood Canal Spot Shrimp.

SMELT FISHERMEN

In the fall the tiny smelt fish come in close to shore to spawn on gently sloping gravelly beaches. As the picture shows it is a popular sport to scoop them up in hand-held nets and take them home for a tasty meal.

ANCIENT FORESTS

Ancient forest areas of Hood Canal are: Lena Lake, Lower Big Quilcene River Trail, Duckabush River, and the upper South Fork Skokomish. For more information on these ancient forests I recommend *Visitors' Guide to Ancient Forests of Western Washington* by the Dittmars: Ann, David, Jane, Tom, Judy and Steve (Washington, D.C.: The Wilderness Society, 1989). The following quote is from their book:

Go back to the woods. Listen to the silence. Breathe deep of the scented air. Stretch your legs where the ground is covered with needles. Stretch your neck to see the tops of giant trees. Look, listen, smell, feel--and experience renewal from the ancient places.

WILCOX MANSION

A curious sight from the water is a large mansion sitting on a bluff just past Tekiu Point. In 1936 at the urging of his wife Colonel Julian Wilcox selected Northwest architect Lionel Pries to design the house. The Colonel's wife and sister-in-law were from high society in San Francisco and their tastes were extravagant. The house and grounds reflect their high tastes. The house had many unique features: Every room in the house is at an angle to capture the spectacular views of the Olympic Mountains and Hood Canal; the kitchen floors were real cork; a special elevator to lift the guests sea chests to the second story guest bedroom, (where Clark Gable once stayed); fluorescent lighting several years before fluorescent lighting was introduced to the nation at the 1939 World's Fair; secret compartments for the Colonel's silver; and photo simulated marble walls more expensive to create than real marble; and an intercom connecting each room with the servants quarters. The grounds featured fish ponds, lush gardens and a bathing pool. The Wilcox House is carrying on its grand tradition of entertainment today as a bread and breakfast house.

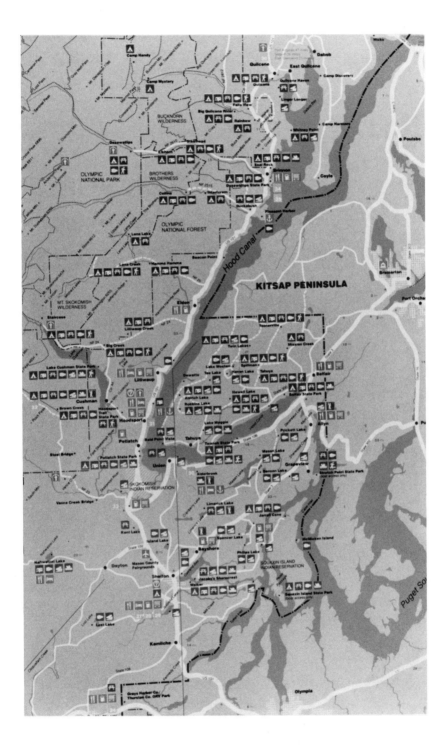

Chapter 8

EXPLORING HOOD CANAL

Each area covered in this chapter is unique and has its own separate personality. It was always with much reluctance that I moved on to explore another area of Hood Canal. When your exploration ends you will already be planning what you will see and do on your next exploration of Hood Canal.

BELFAIR

LOCATION AND DESCRIPTION

Belfair is a small town located at the head of Hood Canal. Belfair is 29.8 miles from Tacoma via State Route 16 west and State Route 3 south and an hour trip from Seattle via the Bremerton ferry and State Route 304 and State Route 3.

FACILITIES

Belfair is a full service town.

THINGS TO DO

Belfair is a good starting point for your "great" circle tour of Hood Canal.

COMMENTS

Belfair, formerly called Clifton, started as a supply town for pioneer loggers, homesteaders, and gold miners.

DEVEREAUX LAKE ACCESS

LOCATION AND DESCRIPTION

From Belfair 3 miles south on State Route 3, east shore.

Washington State Department of Wildlife access to 94 acre Lake Devereaux--1.00 acre with 75 feet waterfront.

FACILITIES

1 lane cement boat launch ramp; 40 parking spaces; fiberglass toilets; no drinking water.

THINGS TO DO

Fishing--Rainbow Trout; Kokanee Salmon.

COMMENTS

Fair to good spring fishing for planted Rainbow Trout with carryovers to five pounds.

PRICKETT--TRAILS END LAKE ACCESS

LOCATION AND DESCRIPTION

From Belfair 4.1 miles west via State Route 106, turn left at Trails End Lake sign unto East Trails Road, 1.5 miles south turn east, road circles lake, site at south end.

Washington State Department of Wildlife access to 74 acre Prickett--Trails End Lake--120 feet waterfront on .54 acres.

FACILITIES

1 lane gravel boat launch ramp; 30 parking spaces; fiberglass toilets; no drinking water.

THINGS TO DO

Fishing--Rainbow Trout.

COMMENTS

Fair for Rainbow Trout up to 10 inches.

MASON LAKE COUNTY PARK AND ACCESS

LOCATION AND DESCRIPTION

From Belfair west on State Route 106 4.1 miles, turn left at Mason Lake County Park sign unto East Trails Road, park at northeast end of lake.

County park on 995 acre Mason Lake. Open all year.

FACILITIES

1 lane boat launch ramp; 12 parking spaces; drinking water; restrooms.

THINGS TO DO

Fishing--Kokanee Salmon; picnicking; swimming.

COMMENTS

The best fishing is in the summer for Kokanee Salmon.

Mason Lake also has a Washington State Department of Wildlife access with a 1 lane boat launch ramp, 30 parking spaces and toilets at the northeast end of lake.

TWANOH STATE PARK--MARINE STATE PARK

LOCATION AND DESCRIPTION

7.6 miles west of Belfair on State Route 106.

180 acre Washington State Park with 3,167 water-front feet on Hood Canal noted for its swimming beach and warm clear saltwater. Seasonal use April 15--September 30; limited day use facilities, including boat launch open year round.

FACILITIES

Concession stand open Memorial Day--Labor Day; 125 picnic sites; 3 kitchenettes, 2 large kitchens with wood stoves (one can be reserved); 580 feet of guarded swimming beach; 47 campsites (fees), 9 of which have hookups; group camp area which can be reserved; showers; facilities for disabled people; tables; stoves; kitchen and picnic shelters; 3 lane boat launch ramp with 25 parking spaces; moorage--11 slips, floats(192 moorage float space footage) and 7 moorage buoys; sewage pumpout station and porta-potty dump station for boaters; tennis court; snack bar; telephone; newspaper machines; playground; public fishing pier with railings; restrooms; horseshoe pits; drinking water; hiking trails; children's wading pool; 2 bath houses.

THINGS TO DO

Boating; swimming; waterskiing; fishing; hiking; shellfish gathering--oysters, clams, crabs (pot fishing); picnicking; camping; smelt dipping.

COMMENTS

The structures within the park were constructed during the depression by the 4728th Company of the Civilian Conservation Corps from Medora, North Dakota. They are made of brick, rock, and wood and are noted for their excellent craftsmanship.

UNION

LOCATION AND DESCRIPTION

Union is a historic town 14.9 miles from Belfair via State Route 106. It is on the south shore of the Great Bend--where Hood Canal turns from south to northeast.

FACILITIES

Union and its adjacent areas along the canal offer the following facilities: marina; transient moorage floats; grocery store; boat launch ramp and hoists; fuel dock; restaurant; post office; fashions boutique; styling salon; cafe; gourmet foods; baskets and gifts; trailer village with hookups; cottages; liquor store; laundromat; hot tub; cabins; boat lift sling; country store; cafe; tavern; Mason County public launching area with 2 hour parking; outboard repair shop; gas station; car repair; RV campgrounds; Union boat launch--1 lane boat launch ramp, with 4 parking spaces.

Alderbrook Resort on the cove 1.9 miles east of Union has a motel, restaurant, 18 hole golf course, yacht club, tennis, pools, spa, swimming and marine facilities.

THINGS TO DO

Boating; fishing.

COMMENTS

The westernmost marina should be approached from the northeast to avoid shoal water and snags.

SKOKOMISH TIDELAND

LOCATION AND DESCRIPTION

From Belfair 16.2 miles west via State Route 106.
Washington State Department of Wildlife saltwater
tideland wildlife area on 104.68 acres off mouth of
Skokomish River (Mason County, Section 06, Township
21N, Range 3W).

FACILITIES

None.

THINGS TO DO

Hunting.

COMMENTS

Tidelands can be used for public shooting only.

HUNTER FARMS PHEASANT RELEASE SITE

LOCATION AND DESCRIPTION

17.8 miles from Belfair via State Route 106. Site is at Hunter Farms east of Skokomish River and north of State Route 106.

Washington State Department of Wildlife pheasant release site.

FACILITIES

Limited parking along State Route 106.

THINGS TO DO

Ring-necked Pheasant hunting.

COMMENTS

The Washington State Department of Wildlife re- leases 600 Ring-necked Pheasants during the season with the majority being released prior to the weekends and holidays.

The birds are raised by the Washington State Department of Wildlife at the Lewis County Game Farm.

SKOKOMISH INDIAN RESERVATION

LOCATION AND DESCRIPTION

The Skokomish Indian Reservation is 18.6 miles from Belfair via State Route 106.

The Skokomish Indian Reservation is made up of 4986.97 acres. The Skokomish River is the eastern and southern boundary of the reservation and empties into Annas Bay on Hood Canal which marks the northwestern boundary. Annas Bay, immediately west of Union is a broad, open bay the eastern half being formed by the river and at low tide extends 0.2 miles into the canal.

FACILITIES

Produce stand; store; gift shop; firework stands; seafood store; salmon stands; church; gas station; grocery; deli; Indian knick knack store; propane store; Tribal Community Center.

THINGS TO DO

Fishing; shopping.

COMMENTS

During the late summer and fall Skokomish Indians fish for returning salmon as they have done for centuries.

BROWN CREEK CAMPGROUND, OLYMPIC NATIONAL FOREST

LOCATION AND DESCRIPTION

From U.S. Highway 101 go 5.6 miles northwest on Skokomish Valley Rd. keeping to right. Drive 9.3 miles north on Forest Service Road 23. Stay to right and go .6 miles east on Forest Service Road 2353. Turn right after going over one lane bridge and drive .4 miles to campground.

U.S. Forest Service campground on Brown Creek. Open year round.

FACILITIES

19 campsites (fees) with no hookups; tables; fire rings; drinking water; vault toilets.

THINGS TO DO

Swimming; fishing; hiking; hunting.

COMMENTS

The Brown Creek Loop Trail #877 is a short family oriented hike around a beaver pond. Starts near campground well.

SMITH--SKOKOMISH RIVER

LOCATION AND DESCRIPTION

From Belfair drive 18.3 miles west via State Route 106. Turn left at Hunter Farms onto Purdy Cut-off Road and drive 2.7 miles to U.S. Highway 101. To reach north bank site drive 1.2 miles north on U.S. Highway 101 across mouth of Skokomish River and take W Sunnyside Rd. to left in the southwest corner of the Skokomish Reservation. Approximately 1.5 miles upstream from U.S. Highway 101. Section 9, Township 21 N, Range 4W.

Washington State Department of Wildlife site--3,060 feet of waterfront on Skokomish River on 65 acres.

FACILITIES

Fiberglass toilets; 1 lane dirt boat launch ramp; 20 parking spaces.

THINGS TO DO

Fishing--winter and some summer steelhead, sea-run Cutthroat, Whitefish, Dolly Varden Trout, Coho and Chinook Salmon.

COMMENTS

Good spot to take out a driftboat.

SKOKOMISH RIVER ACCESS--OLD BRIDGE SITE

LOCATION AND DESCRIPTION

Drive north on U.S. Highway 101 across mouth of Skokomish River and take road to left. Approximately .7 mile upstream. Site on south side of river. Section 16, Township 21 N, Range 4 W.

Washington State Department of Wildlife access to Skokomish River--1.46 acres and 60 feet waterfront.

FACILITIES

1 lane dirt boat launch ramp.

THINGS TO DO

Fishing—winter and some summer steelhead, sea-run Cutthroat Trout, Whitefish, Dolly Varden, Coho and Chinook Salmon.

COMMENTS

The Skokomish River is considered the biggest and the best of the Hood Canal rivers for fishing.

POTLATCH STATE PARK--MARINE STATE PARK

LOCATION AND DESCRIPTION

Potlatch State Park is located on the west side of the canal on Annas Bay on The Great Bend, where Hood Canal turns northeast. The park is 22 miles from Belfair via State Route 106 and U.S. Highway 101.

Washington State Park on Hood Canal.

FACILITIES

18 full hook-up sites, 17 standard tent sites, and 2 primitive sites for bicyclists and hikers (fees); dump station; showers; tables; stoves; 5 moorage buoys; playfield; picnic shelter; restrooms; public boat launch 3/4 miles north of the park; drinking water.

THINGS TO DO

Boating; shellfish gathering--oysters, mussels, cockles, clams, crabs, and shrimp; fishing; hiking; scuba diving; picnicking; swimming; watch for animals and birds.

COMMENTS

In times past this has been the sight of Indian potlatches, a resort, and a lumbermill. The park is still used by native American Indians for social gatherings.

POTLATCH

LOCATION AND DESCRIPTION

Potlatch is a small town 23 miles from Belfair via State Route 106 and U.S. Highway 101. It is on the west side of the canal about 2 miles south of Hoodsport and opposite The Great Bend, where Hood Canal turns northeast.

FACILITIES

Potlatch and its adjacent areas along the canal offer the following facilities: RV park; laundromat; propane; camping; gift shop; store; bait; wood; restrooms; hamburger stand; restaurant; mobile home park; diner; resort; waterfront RV pads with full hookups; car wash; ice; motorcycle parts and accessories; telephone; diving center--sales, service, air rental; marine store--motors, boat sales, supplies, repair.

Cushman Park--Hood Canal Recreational Park--boat launch; telephone; restrooms; picnic tables; parking.

THINGS TO DO

Boating; shellfish gathering--clams, crabpots; fishing; swimming; picnicking; observe hydroelectric plant.

COMMENTS

Old generator parts are on display at Cushman Park.

HOODSPORT--PORT OF HOODSPORT

LOCATION AND DESCRIPTION

Hoodsport is the largest town along the shores of Hood Canal and is 24.9 miles from Belfair via State Route 106 and U.S. Highway 101. It is on the west shore 4 miles southwest of Dewatto.

FACILITIES

Gift shops; restaurants; motels; Port of Hoodsport transient moorage--10 slips (moorage time limit); marina--sling launch, floats (depths to 24'), repair facilities and marine supplies; grocery store; gas stations; scuba air fills; fastfood; seafood market; winery tasting room; trailer park; Hood Canal Ranger District Office, U.S. Forest Service--information, maps; hardware store; public restrooms; barber shop; beauty shop; market--drugs, miscellaneous, groceries, ice cream; cafe; video store; tavern; bank, liquor store; library; dentist; post office; towing; auto center; resort; RV park--motel, spa house, dock; public fishing pier with parking; saltwater park--2 lane boat launch ramp, 20 parking spaces, drinking water, restrooms.

THINGS TO DO

Boating; fishing; shrimping; scuba diving; visit Washington State Department of Fisheries Hood Canal

Salmon Hatchery; visit Hood Canal Ranger District Office, U.S. Forest Service.

LOWER CUSHMAN--KOKANEE LAKE ACCESS

LOCATION AND DESCRIPTION

From Hoodsport, 2.8 miles west, then 1 mile south, site on southeast side.

Washington State Department of Wildlife access to 450 acre Kokanee Lake--4.40 acres with 323' waterfront.

FACILITIES

1 lane gravel boat launch ramp; 100 parking spaces; fiberglass toilets; no drinking water.

THINGS TO DO

Fishing--Cutthroat Trout, Kokanee Salmon, Rainbow Trout.

COMMENTS

Good early-season Cutthroat Trout fishing and good summer fishing for Kokanee Salmon.

LAKE CUSHMAN STATE PARK

LOCATION AND DESCRIPTION

7.1 miles northwest of Hoodsport on Lake Cushman Road.

565 acre Washington State Park with 41,500 waterfront feet on 4000 acre Lake Cushman. Lake Cushman is a 10 mile long man made reservoir surrounded by the Olympic Mountains.

FACILITIES

50 standard campsites, 30 full hookup campsites and 2 primitive walk-in campsites (fees); dumpstation; restroom; showers; tables; stoves; 3 lane boat launch ramp with 48 parking spaces; moorage; primitive sites for bikers and hikers; kitchen shelter; facilities for disabled; drinking water; group camp which can be reserved; picnic area; day use shelter with electricity; unguarded swimming beach.

THINGS TO DO

Boating; fishing--Cutthroat Trout, Kokanee Salmon, Rainbow Trout; Dolly Varden Trout, and a very small number of unique landlocked King Salmon; hiking; water-skiing; picnicking; swimming; mushroom gathering; golfing nearby; tour Lake Cushman Dam facility.

COMMENTS

In 1920 the City of Tacoma was granted a lease to construct a dam on Lake Cushman to generate power. The dam, considered an engineering marvel, was completed in 1926 and increased the size of the lake from 400 acres to 4,000 acres.

HOODSPORT TRAIL STATE PARK

LOCATION AND DESCRIPTION

3 miles west of Hoodsport on Lake Cushman Road.
Washington State park--80 wooded acres bordering Dow Creek.

FACILITIES

3 picnic table sites; vault toilet; 5 parking stalls; 2 miles of trails with two foot bridges over Dow Creek.

THINGS TO DO

Hiking; picnicking; fishing.

COMMENTS

Park was formerly mule barn and staging area for the Hoodsport Ranger District. Supplies were sent from here to areas in the National Forest. Remnants of the barn and the foundation can still be seen.

BIG CREEK CAMPGROUND, OLYMPIC NATIONAL FOREST

LOCATION AND DESCRIPTION

Travel U.S. Highway 101 to Hoodsport and turn left unto Lake Cushman Road. Drive 9.2 miles to Forest Service Road 24. Turn left and travel 100 yards. Big Creek Campground is on right hand side of road.

U.S. Forest Service campground on Big Creek. Open year round.

FACILITIES

23 campsites with no hookups (fees); dump station; showers; tables; fire rings; drinking water; vault toilets.

THINGS TO DO

Swimming; fishing; hiking; mountain climbing; boating; jogging; watch for animals and birds; nature walk.

COMMENTS

The 1.1 mile Big Creek Campground Loop Trail #827 is an excellent trail for jogging.

STAIRCASE   CAMPGROUND,   OLYMPIC   NATIONAL PARK

LOCATION AND DESCRIPTION

15.8 miles northwest of Hoodsport via Lake Cushman Road and Forest Service Road 24.

Olympic National Forest campground on North Fork of Skokomish River. Open all year.

FACILITIES

60 campsites with no hookups (fees); amphitheatre; drinking water; restrooms; facilities for disabled. Recommended trailer length 16'.

THINGS TO DO

Fishing; hiking; picnicking; summer naturalist program.

COMMENTS

Staircase got its name from a section of trail called the "Devil's Staircase". It was named this because the trail going over a rock hill was so steep the only footholds in certain sections were small logs fastened to the rocks. In 1911 miners blasted a wide level trail across the face of this rock hill and this trail is still being used and is called Shady Lane.

HOODSPORT BEACH   DNR BEACH 43

LOCATION AND DESCRIPTION

Just north of Hoodsport on U.S. Highway 101.

Washington State Department of Natural Resources saltwater beach--2,951 foot cobble beach below roadway.

FACILITIES

Limited parking along U.S. Highway 101.

THINGS TO DO

Shellfish gathering--Common Pacific Littleneck Clams, Horse Clams, Butter Clams, Blue Mussels, Red Crab.

COMMENTS

Do not trespass on surrounding private beach; accessible by boat and car.

SUNDE ROCK

LOCATION AND DESCRIPTION

2 miles south of Lilliwaup.
Offshore rock and underwater ledges.

FACILITIES

Parking.

THINGS TO DO

Scuba diving.

OCTOPUS HOLE

LOCATION AND DESCRIPTION

3/4 miles north of Hoodsport and 1 1/4 miles south of Lilliwaup.
Underwater rock ledge in 30 feet of water.

FACILITIES

Parking.

THINGS TO DO

Scuba diving.

LILLIWAUP

LOCATION AND DESCRIPTION

Lilliwaup is a village 29.1 miles from Belfair via State Route 106 and U.S. Highway 101. It is on a small shallow cove on the west shore of Hood Canal about six miles southwest of Eldon.

FACILITIES

Post office; motel; general store; gas pumps; barber shop.

About 1 mile south--resort with berths, electricity, gas, diesel fuel, water, ice, marine supplies, 1 1/2 ton elevator for hull and engine repair for boats up to 19'.

THINGS TO DO

Boating; fishing; shellfish gathering.

COMMENTS

Lilliwaup has excellent viewing of many species of birds right from your car.

LILLIWAUP TIDELANDS

LOCATION AND DESCRIPTION

1/2 mile north of Lilliwaup.
Washington State Parks and Recreation Commission
park lands on Hood Canal consisting of 4,122 waterfront
feet of tidelands. Beach-mix.

FACILITIES

Parking.

THINGS TO DO

Shellfish gathering--oysters, clams; scuba diving.

EAGLE CREEK RECREATIONAL TIDELANDS

LOCATION AND DESCRIPTION

North of Lilliwaup.
Tidelands.

FACILITIES

Parking.

THINGS TO DO

Shellfish gathering--clams, crabs, oysters.

MELBOURNE RECREATION CAMP

LOCATION AND DESCRIPTION
Start on U.S. Highway 101. Take Jorsted Creek Road
(Forest Service Road 24) 5.5 miles. Turn left (gravel,
one lane) and go 1.8 miles. Keep left for 0.7 mile to
camp.

Washington State Department of Natural Resources 5 acre campground on 35 acre Melbourne Lake.

FACILITIES

5 campsites; outhouse toilets.

THINGS TO DO

Fishing--Cutthroat Trout.

COMMENTS

Melbourne Lake will remind you of Alaska. Good to excellent fishing for Cutthroat Trout up to 14 inches. Fall fishing is best.

LILLIWAUP CREEK RECREATIONAL CAMP

LOCATION AND DESCRIPTION

Start on U.S. Highway 101. Take Jorsted Creek Road (Forest Service Road 24, gravel one lane). Go 6.8 miles. Camp on right.

10 acre Washington State Department of Natural Resources campground on Lilliwaup Creek.

FACILITIES

13 campsites with no hookups; tables; stoves; toilets, drinking water.

THINGS TO DO

Camping; picnicking.

COMMENTS

There is an interesting educational sign about forest renewal pointing out actual examples taking place at the camp.

ELDON

LOCATION AND DESCRIPTION

Eldon is a west shore settlement 36.8 miles from Belfair via State Route 106 and U.S. Highway 101. It is on the south and north banks of the Hamma Hamma River about 3 miles southwest of Holly. The Hamma Hamma River estuary extends 0.5 miles from shore.

FACILITIES

Seafood store; picnic area; Indian art gallery; store; gas station; laundromat; restaurant; telephone; propane.

THINGS TO DO

Dining; picnicing; shopping.

COMMENTS

Unmarked jetties from the river out unto the mud flats on Hood Canal are a hazard to small craft.
Albert Pfundt, Holly pioneer now deceased, caught an octopus north of the Hamma Hamma River measuring 25 feet from tip to tip.

HAMMA HAMMA CAMPGROUND, OLYMPIC NATIONAL FOREST

LOCATION AND DESCRIPTION

2.4 miles north of Eldon on U.S. Highway 101 and 6 miles west on Forest Service Road 25.
U.S. Forest Service campground on Hamma Hamma River in Olympic National Forest.

FACILITIES

15 campsites with no hookups (fees); tables; fire rings; fresh water; vault toilets.

THINGS TO DO

Fishing; hiking; mountain climbing; hunting.

LENA CREEK CAMPGROUND, OLYMPIC NATIONAL FOREST

LOCATION AND DESCRIPTION

2.4 miles north of Eldon on U.S. Highway 101 and 7.7 miles west on Forest Service Road 25.
U.S. Forest Service campground on Lena Creek in the Olympic National Forest.

FACILITIES

12 campsites with no hookups (fees); tables; fresh water; fire rings; vault toilets.

THINGS TO DO

Fishing; hiking; mountain climbing; hunting.

COMMENTS

The campground is next to the Lena Lake trailhead. Lena Lake is west of the campground and is a beautiful hike through portions of virgin forest.

TRITON COVE STATE PARK

LOCATION AND DESCRIPTION

Triton Cove State Park is 5.9 miles north of Eldon.

28.4 acres with 555 feet of waterfront and tidelands.

FACILITIES

Boat launch ramp; dock with 2 floats each measuring 10 feet by 30 feet; campsites; restroom.

THINGS TO DO

Boating; fishing; camping.

COMMENTS

The Washington State Parks and Recreation Commission has plans for Triton Cove State Park to become a full service park with boat launch, day use and campground facilities.

TRITON

LOCATION AND DESCRIPTION

Triton is a resort area north of Eldon. Just north of Triton is a low, rocky, timbered point called Triton Head with a reef that extends 200 yards from the point at low tide.

FACILITIES

Two resorts; berths; gasoline; diesel fuel; water; ice; dry storage; marine supplies; hoist and railways to 10 tons; outboard engine repair.

THINGS TO DO

Shellfish gathering--crabs (pot fishing).

COMMENTS

The stakes and brush mark oyster beds on the flat which extends off the mouth of Fulton Creek to the north of Triton Head.

Triton Cove formed by Triton Head and the west shore is a good anchorage against southern winds.

COLLINS CAMPGROUND, OLYMPIC NATIONAL FOREST

LOCATION AND DESCRIPTION

Approximately 22.2 miles north of Hoodsport on U.S. Highway 101 and 5 miles west on the Duckabush River Road, Forest Service Road 2510.

U.S. Forest Service campground on Duckabush River. Open year round.

FACILITIES

16 campsites with no hookups (fees); tables; drinking water; fire rings; vault toilets.

THINGS TO DO

Swimming; fishing; hiking trails; horseback riding; hunting; river walks.

COMMENTS

The Duckabush Trailhead is located approximately 1 mile west of Collins Campground. 7 1/2 miles from the trailhead, 100 yards past 2nd stream crossing within park on southeast side of the trail is the largest living Grand Fir (*Abies grandis*) tree with a circumference of 229 inches, height of 251 feet and a spread of 43 feet.

PLEASANT HARBOR MARINE PARK

LOCATION AND DESCRIPTION

23.2 miles north of Hoodsport and 2 miles south of Brinnon via U.S. Highway 101.

Washington State Marine Park on .84 acres with 100 feet of waterfront on Pleasant Harbor. Pleasant Harbor is a small cove 300 yards wide with a narrow entrance on the west shore of Hood Canal about 3 miles west of Misery Point.

FACILITIES

Pier, moorage floats--218 moorage float space footage(8 slips); pit toilets.

Adjacent to private full service marina-- berths, electricity, gasoline, water, ice, limited marine supplies, swimming pool

THINGS TO DO

Boating; fishing; shellfish gathering--clams, oysters.

COMMENTS

Entering Pleasant Harbor stay in midchannel until clear of 6 foot shoal.

Pleasant Harbor offers secure anchorage in all weather in a depth of about 36 feet with a mud bottom.

DOSEWALLIPS STATE PARK

LOCATION AND DESCRIPTION

25.2 miles north of Hoodsport and 2 miles south of Brinnon on Hood Canal via U.S. Highway 101.

514 acres on Dosewallips River and Hood Canal at the foot of the Olympic Mountains with views of Mt. Walker and Mt. Constance. Dosewallips State Park was formerly the site of several homesteads and was called Dose Meadows.

FACILITIES

129 campsites with 40 having hookups and 2 primitive sites for hikers and bicyclists (fees); dumpstation; facilities for disabled; restrooms; hot showers; tables and stoves; picnic sites and large parking area for day visitors; two group camp areas which can be reserved by writing any time after second Monday in January to Dosewallips State Park, P.O. Box K, Brinnon, Wa. 98320.

THINGS TO DO

Hiking; picnicking; fishing--salmon and steelhead in Dosewallips River, salmon and large variety of bottom fish in Hood Canal; wildlife watching--deer, Elk, Racoons, Beavers, skunks, seals, Bald Eagles, waterfowl, and other wildlife.

COMMENTS

The name "Dosewallips" originates from "Dos-wail-opsh", the name of a legendary Twana Indian who was turned into a mountain, forming the source of the Dosewallips River.

BRINNON

LOCATION AND DESCRIPTION

Brinnon is a small village 50.7 miles from Belfair via State Route 106 and U.S. Highway 101. It is on the south side of the Dosewallips River and 3.5 miles west of Oak Head, at the entrance of Dabob Bay.

FACILITIES

General store (fishing and camping supplies) with gas pumps and propane; post office; restaurant; motel; senior citizen center; water and ice; ambulance service; churches.

THINGS TO DO

Enjoy nearby Dosewallips State Park and Seal Rock Campgrounds.

COMMENTS

You may be able to sight a Trident submarine doing tests in Dabob Bay from Brinnon.

ELKHORN CAMPGROUND, OLYMPIC NATIONAL FOREST

LOCATION AND DESCRIPTION

10.8 miles northwest from U.S. Highway 101 at Brinnon. Drive the Dosewallips Road to gravel Forest Service Road 2610 to the campground.

U.S. Forest Service campground in old-growth wooded area on the north bank of the Dosewallips River. Open May thru October.

FACILITIES

20 campsites with no hookups (fees); tables; firepits; freshwater; vault toilets.

THINGS TO DO

Fishing; hiking; camping; picnicking; watch for animals and birds.

COMMENTS

All varieties of berries found in the Hood Canal area are present at Elkhorn.

DOSEWALLIPS CAMPGROUND, OLYMPIC NATIONAL PARK

LOCATION AND DESCRIPTION

From Brinnon 1.5 miles north via U.S. Highway 101 and 14.5 miles west on Forest Service Road 2610.

Olympic National Park campground along Dosewallips River. Closed October through May.

FACILITIES

33 campsites for tents only (no fee); tables; facilities for disabled; restrooms; drinking water.

THINGS TO DO

Fishing; hiking; picnicking; camping on Dosewallips River; nature trails; summer naturalist program.

COMMENTS

The gravel road to the Dosewallips Campground is narrow and steep with precipitous dropoffs and rock overhangs and towing a trailer on this road is not recommended.

SEAL ROCK CAMPGROUND, OLYMPIC NATIONAL FOREST

LOCATION AND DESCRIPTION

1 mile north of Brinnon on U.S. Highway 101.

U.S. Forest Service campground on Hood Canal with beautiful views of Hood Canal and the mountains to the southeast. Open May thru October.

FACILITIES

41 campsites with no hookups (fees); tables; firepits; swimming; restrooms; drinking water; telephone; hand boat launch; facilities for the disabled.

THINGS TO DO

Boating; fishing; shellfish gathering--clams, crab, shrimp, oysters; beachcombing; birdwatching; picnicking; swimming; scuba diving.

COMMENTS

You can take a self guided tour along a trail through the forest and signs will explain the Indian way of life and his relationship to his surroundings.

PT. WHITNEY TIDELANDS AND SHELLFISH LABORATORY

LOCATION AND DESCRIPTION

3.2 miles north of Brinnon on U.S. Highway 101. Turn right at sign.

Washington State Department of Fisheries shellfish laboratory and saltwater research lagoon and tidelands.

FACILITIES

Visitor center; 1 lane boat launch ramp; fishing pier with railings; restrooms; 5 parking spaces; drinking water.

THINGS TO DO

Boating; visitors interpretive center; shellfish gathering--oysters, clams.

COMMENTS

The Pt. Whitney Shellfish Laboratory has done pioneering research on oyster and geoduck reproduction.

RAINBOW CAMPGROUND, OLYMPIC NATIONAL FOREST

LOCATION AND DESCRIPTION

6.6 miles north of Brinnon on U.S. Highway 101.

U.S. Forest Service campground in area of heavily wooded old-growth and new-growth trees along with wildflowers, huckleberry plants and spring blooming Pacific Rhododendrons. Campground open all year.

FACILITIES

9 campsites with tables and firepits (no fee); fresh water; vault toilets.

THINGS TO DO

Camping; picnicking; hiking.

COMMENTS

The Rainbow Canyon Trail is a short trail leading to scenic views of the Big Quilcene River and a small picturesque waterfall and pool.

FALLS VIEW CAMPGROUND, OLYMPIC NATIONAL FOREST

LOCATION AND DESCRIPTION

8.1 miles north of Brinnon on U.S. Highway 101.
U.S. Department of Agriculture campground in mountains above the Big Quilcene River. Open May thru September.

FACILITIES

30 campsites with no hookups (fees); tables; firepits; fresh water; vault toilets, including a disabled facility.

THINGS TO DO

Hiking; scenic vista; camping; picnicking; fishing.

COMMENTS

Short 0.1 mile vista trail has views of waterfall, Big Quilcene River far below, and mountains.
The Falls View Canyon Trail (0.6 mile) leads to the bottom of the canyon and the Big Quilcene River.

QUILCENE RIVER ACCESS

LOCATION AND DESCRIPTION

North of Brinnon via U.S. Highway 101.
Washington State Department of Wildlife access to Quilcene River--5,500 feet of riverfront on 4 acres.

FACILITIES

Parking; fiberglass toilets.

THINGS TO DO

Fishing; hiking.

QUILCENE

LOCATION AND DESCRIPTION

11.2 miles north of Brinnon via U.S. Highway 101.

Pioneer logging community now famous for Quilcene oysters, near the head of Quilcene Bay, on the west side of Hood Canal.

FACILITIES

Grocery store; gas stations; restaurants; bank; laundromat.

Quilcene Boat Haven (2 miles south of Quilcene on Linger Longer Road)--1 lane boat launch ramp, fuel dock, transient moorage, restrooms, drinking water, showers, picnic tables, fireplaces, 10 parking spaces, swimming beach; Quilcene Ranger District Office, U.S. Forest Service--information, maps, public restrooms.

Jefferson County Campground--shelter, campsites, outhouse.

THINGS TO DO

Boating; picnicking; swimming.

COMMENTS

At Jefferson County Campground a Best 60 is on display--one of first tractors used in logging and forerunner of caterpillar tractor.

DABOB

LOCATION AND DESCRIPTION

From Quilcene stay to the right and head north
taking the Center Road for 4.0 miles. Turn right unto
Dabob Road and go 2.0 miles to Dabob Post Office
Road and drive to end of road.

In pioneer days Dabob was the site of a school and
post office. Dabob is now oyster farming country.

FACILITIES

None.

THINGS TO DO

Observe natural estuary and bird life; Observe oyster
farming: racks for growing of seed, small plant for bag-
ging oyster shells, tanks for growing oyster seed, oyster
beds.

COMMENTS

Beautiful drive along Tarboo Bay on Dabob Post
Office Road. Good viewing of Great Blue Herons at low
tide.

COYLE

LOCATION AND DESCRIPTION

From Dabob turn right off of Dabob Post Office Road unto Dabob--Coyle Road and drive 13.1 miles south to Coyle. You will know you are at Coyle when you see the sign that says Coyle, elevation 300 feet, population 127. In pioneer days Coyle was the site of a post office.

FACILITIES

Fire station; county waste disposal site.

THINGS TO DO

Scenic drive.

COMMENTS

The drive to Coyle takes you through some of the most remote and scenic areas of Hood Canal.

THORNDYKE

LOCATION AND DESCRIPTION

From Coyle drive north on Dabob-Coyle Road 5.4 miles and turn right unto Thorndyke Road and drive 2.6 miles.

Thorndyke was the site of an early schoolhouse for pioneer children.

FACILITIES

None.

THINGS TO DO

Scenic drive.

COMMENTS

Thorndyke Bay is a natural unspoiled estuary owned by Pope Resources and is off limits to the public. It is used by Pope Resources as a duck hunting preserve for their clients--many who are Japanese. It is patrolled and guarded by a caretaker.

SOUTH POINT

LOCATION AND DESCRIPTION

Follow Thorndyke Road to South Point Road and turn right and drive 1.5 miles to end of road.

South Point was the east side ferry terminal of the Lofall-South Point Ferry run across Hood Canal before the floating bridge was built and again from 1979-1982 when the Hood Canal Bridge was being rebuilt.

FACILITIES

Large parking lot, formerly parking lot for ferry traffic, now used by trailers and RV's; tavern with propane gas and microwave food.

THINGS TO DO

Scuba diving; shellfish gathering.

COMMENTS

The sand spit at South Point is highly developed with homes, docks and a private marina. The second sand spit is not developed.

SHINE

LOCATION AND DESCRIPTION

From Thorndyke Road continue south 1.5 miles to State Route 104. Turn right. Drive east .5 miles to Shine Rd. and turn right.

In pioneer days Shine was the site of a schoolhouse and an area of early homesteads. Shine is now a small rural community.

FACILITIES

William R. Hicks County Park.

THINGS TO DO

Scenic view; sightseeing.

COMMENTS

Shine has a perfect southern exposure and faces Squamish Harbor, which is probably how it got its name--the sun always seems to be shining or reflecting off Squamish Harbor. This perfect exposure led to the pioneers planting orchards which can still be seen throughout the area and Shines reputation for growing huckleberries, blackberries, and strawberries.

WILLIAM R. HICKS COUNTY PARK (JEFFERSON COUNTY)

LOCATION

From west end of Hood Canal Floating Bridge turn south unto Shine Road and drive 1.2 miles.

Park along shore of Hood Canal with scenic views of Hood Canal and Olympic Mountains.

FACILITIES

1 lane boat launch ramp; tables and stove; 5 parking spaces; pit toilet; no drinking water.

THINGS TO DO

Boating; shellfish gathering--crabs; picnicking.

COMMENTS

Park is exposed to southerlies.

WOLFE PROPERTY

LOCATION AND DESCRIPTION

The Wolfe Property (includes Shine Tidelands) is located just north of the west end of the Hood Canal Floating Bridge. At west end of Hood Canal Floating Bridge turn right and then make an immediate right onto Termination Point Road and left at Y to park entrance.

Washington State Parks and Recreation Commission park lands on Hood Canal consisting of 134.6 acres with 16,092 feet of tidelands extending from the Hood Canal Floating Bridge along Bywater Bay to the northern boundary of Wolfe property where the spit joins unto Hood Head Island.

FACILITIES

Boat launch ramp; parking; 20 primitive sites (fees); vault toilets; interpretive board; no drinking water.

THINGS TO DO

Boating; shellfish gathering--oysters, clams, crabs; beachcombing; fishing; hiking; camping; skin diving; windsurfing.

COMMENTS

The area is heavily used by clamdiggers and crabbers on most low tides during the summer.

HOOD CANAL FLOATING BRIDGE PUBLIC FISHING ACCESS

LOCATION AND DESCRIPTION

East end of Hood Canal Bridge.

Washington State Department of Fisheries access to bridge pontoons.

FACILITIES

Lights; railings; restrooms; parking; rain cover.

THINGS TO DO

Saltwater fishing.

SALISBURY POINT COUNTY PARK (KITSAP COUNTY)

LOCATION AND DESCRIPTION

1/2 mile northeast of turnoff for Hood Canal Floating Bridge on State Route 3. Left on Wheeler Street, follow signs.

Park with driftwood strewn sand and gravel beach along shores of Hood Canal with views of Hood Canal Floating Bridge and Olympic Mountains.

FACILITIES

1 lane boat launch ramp; tables and stoves; shelter with sink; 25 parking spaces; drinking water; restrooms; big toy for kids.

THINGS TO DO

Boating; swimming; hiking; picnicking.

PORT GAMBLE

LOCATION AND DESCRIPTION

1 mile east of Hood Canal Floating Bridge on State Route 104.
Historic New England style mill town founded in 1853, which is a national historic site.

FACILITIES

Country store; park area with picnic tables; museum.

THINGS TO DO

Sightseeing; picnicking.

COMMENTS

You can take a self guided tour of Port Gamble because all the points of interest and buildings have signs with explanations. Be sure to visit the museum and general store.

PORT GAMBLE INDIAN RESERVATION

LOCATION AND DESCRIPTION

From Port Gamble drive east on State Route 104 4.1 miles. At light turn left and continue on State Route 104 1.4 miles. Turn left onto Hansville Road NE and drive 2.0 miles. Turn left on NE Little Boston Rd.

1,232 acre reservation for Klallam Indians.

FACILITIES

Store; gas station; smoke shop.

THINGS TO DO

Sightseeing.

COMMENTS

The totem pole located past the tribal center has an interesting explanation of the creatures carved on the pole.

FOULWEATHER BLUFF WILDLIFE PRESERVE

LOCATION AND DESCRIPTION

From Hansville Road NE turn left onto Twin Spits Road NE and drive 3 miles. Look for a small turnout on the south side of the road 800 feet east of the Skunk Bay Road intersection (right after red fire hydrant on left). A sign marking trailhead is nailed to a tree. A short hike leads to the preserve. You can see preserve with lagoon from highway--trails right past that.

93 acre wildlife preserve on Hood Canal with scenic views of Hood Canal and Olympic Mountains. The preserve is owned by the Nature Conservancy.

FACILITIES

None.

The southern spit of nearby Twin Spits--two long low points, 0.5 mile and 1 mile south of Foulweather Bluff, has a small resort, gasoline, a marine railway for small-craft, ice and some marine supplies.

THINGS TO DO

Hiking; beachcombing; birdwatching.

COMMENTS

You may want to explore this preserve while waiting for calmer weather before rounding Foulweather Bluff. You can anchor in 50 feet 1 mile southeast of the south spit, in a bight known locally as Races Cove. Colvos Rocks light will be slightly clear of the end of the south point of Twin Spits.

KITSAP MEMORIAL STATE PARK

LOCATION AND DESCRIPTION

2.9 miles south of Hood Canal Floating Bridge on State Route 3. Turn right at Kitsap Memorial State Park sign.

57.63 acre State Park with a 1,797 foot saltwater beach and views of Olympic Mountains.

FACILITIES

51 campsites (no hookups, fees); dumpstation; showers; tables; stoves; kitchen and picnic shelter; 2 moorage buoys; baseball field; horseshoe pits; facilities for disabled; drinking water; restrooms.

THINGS TO DO

Boating; fishing; hiking; baseball field; horseshoe pits; community hall; shellfish gathering--oysters, clams.

COMMENTS

This park is a popular gathering place for the local Scandinavian population many of whose forefathers were pioneer homesteaders.

LOFALL

LOCATION AND DESCRIPTION

3.2 miles from Hood Canal Floating Bridge. Turn right onto Lofall Road and right on Wesley NW Highway.

Residential community--former pioneer community.

FACILITIES

None.

THINGS TO DO

Kitsap Memorial State Park is right next to Lofall.

COMMENTS

Former terminal for Hood Canal Ferry.

BREIDABLICK

LOCATION AND DESCRIPTION

3.9 miles south of Hood Canal Floating Bridge--State Route 3 and Pioneer Way.

Former pioneer community with church and school. The chapel is still used and is surrounded by well maintained farmland and pioneer houses.

FACILITIES

Gas station; building supply; food mart; restrooms; diesel fuel; large parking area.

THINGS TO DO

Sightseeing.

COMMENTS

Scandinavian names on tombstones are a testimony to the role the Scandinavian pioneers played in settling this area--Olsen, Bjornstad, Berglund, Halvorson, Larson, etc.

BANGOR

LOCATION AND DESCRIPTION

From Hood Canal Floating Bridge drive south on State Route 3 16.3 miles and take Newbury Hill Road exit. Turn right at Provost Rd. and drive 1.3 miles to N.W. Anderson Hill Rd. Turn left and drive 1.1 miles to Olympic View Rd. N.W. Turn right onto Olympic View Rd. N.W. and drive 4.5 miles to Bangor.

Bangor is a quaint little community right along Hood Canal. North boundary of Bangor is security fence for Trident Naval Submarine Base.

FACILITIES

None.

THINGS TO DO

Sightseeing.

COMMENTS

Much of the history of Bangor is still visible--the old Goodwin general store, the old schoolhouse now converted to a residence, and the few remaining pilings on the spit where the old canal steamer used to land. The floating clam factory is long gone and most of the community was taken over by the military base but I think you will agree Bangor and the surrounding countryside with its old farmhouses still has a special charm.

SEABECK

LOCATION AND DESCRIPTION

From Bangor turn right off of Olympic View Rd. N.W. onto N.W. Anderson Hill Rd. and drive 2.7 miles to Seabeck Highway N.W. Drive 2.7 miles to Seabeck.

Seabeck is a settlement and resort at the head of Seabeck Bay--a small cove on the east shore of Hood Canal.

FACILITIES

Marina; boat launch (hoist); boat rental shop; transient moorage floats; bait shop; fuel dock; general store; restaurant; fast food restaurant; post office.

THINGS TO DO

Boating; fishing; scuba diving; shellfish gathering--crabs (pot fishing).

COMMENTS

Seabeck is exposed to northerly winds and in a severe storm in 1991 the entire marina was destroyed.

Seabeck was the former terminal for the Hood Canal ferry from Brinnon.

The former lumbermill site and some of its buildings is now the home for a Bible conference center.

MISERY POINT   ACCESS

LOCATION AND DESCRIPTION

2.0 miles northwest of Seabeck. Follow signs from Seabeck.

Washington State Department of Wildlife access to Hood Canal--4.20 acres with 100 feet of waterfront.

FACILITIES

1 lane cement boat launch ramp; parking; fiberglass toilets.

THINGS TO DO

Boating; fishing.

SCENIC BEACH STATE PARK

LOCATION AND DESCRIPTION

1.8 miles northwest of Seabeck. Follow signs from Seabeck.

State park with 90 acres of forestland and 1600 foot saltwater beach noted for its scenic views of the Olympic Mountains. Originally "Scenic Beach" was the name of a fishing and hunting resort run by Joe Emel, Sr., a local pioneer.

FACILITIES

52 campsites with no hookups (fees), eighteen are pull-through sites with 4 double or "buddy" sites; dump-station; showers; facilities for disabled; tables; stoves; kitchen; shelter; drinking water; restrooms with hot water and showers; play area; horseshoe pits; fire rings; 78 picnic sites; volleyball courts; bathhouse with showers; facilities for boating and scuba diving. Public boat launch one mile north at Misery Point.

THINGS TO DO

Boating; shellfish gathering--oysters; fishing; trails; swimming; animal and bird watching--Raccoons, squirrels, Black-tailed Deer, grouse, towhees, thrushes, wrens, Pileated Woodpecker, waterfowl.

COMMENTS

Be sure to see the historic Emel House.

CAMP UNION

LOCATION AND DESCRIPTION

Head south from Seabeck and take the Seabeck-Holly Road 3.1 miles and turn left unto Holly Road and drive .5 miles.

Former logging camp with its original buildings still being used commercially and some of its residents still living in the old camp cabins.

FACILITIES

Restaurant; gas station; grocery store.

THINGS TO DO

Sightseeing.

COMMENTS

Logging trestle ruins can still be seen across road from town.

1876 ~ 1970
ALBERT PFUNDT
A DEVOTED and DEDICATED
HOLLY PIONEER WHO WAS
LOVED BY ALL

HOLLY

LOCATION AND DESCRIPTION

From Seabeck take Seabeck-Holly Road N.W. 10.2 miles to Holly.

Holly is a small settlement on Hood Canal with a fantastic view across canal of the Olympic Mountains. Many of the descendants of the early pioneers still live here.

FACILITIES

None.

THINGS TO DO

Sightseeing.

COMMENTS

For many years pioneer Albert Pfundt operated a resort at Holly renting out cabins and boats to tourists in the summer.

HAVEN LAKE ACCESS

LOCATION AND DESCRIPTION

From Belfair 3.6 miles west on State Route 300. Turn right on Belfair Tahuya Rd. becoming Haven Way and go 5.7 miles. Turn left on Rhododendron Blvd. and drive .1 mile and turn right and go .1 mile.

Washington State Department of Wildlife public access area to 65 acre Haven Lake--116 feet of waterfront on 1.15 acres.

FACILITIES

1 lane boat launch; 20 parking spaces; fiberglass toilets.

THINGS TO DO

Fishing--Rainbow Trout; boating; waterskiing.

COMMENTS

Fishing is good to excellent for Rainbow Trout up to 12 inches long.

WOOTEN LAKE ACCESS

LOCATION AND DESCRIPTION

From Belfair 3.6 miles west on State Route 300. Turn right on Belfair Tahuya Rd. becoming Haven Way and go 6.5 miles to Mtn. View Dr. Turn left and drive .1 mile.

Washington State Department of Wildlife public access area to 68 acre Wooten Lake-- 45 feet of waterfront on 0.56 acres. Lake has cabins built around it.

FACILITIES

Parking; fiberglass toilets; 1 lane boat launch ramp; 60 parking spaces.

THINGS TO DO

Fishing--Rainbow Trout, Cutthroat Trout.

COMMENTS

Fair to good fishing for Rainbow Trout up to 10 inches and some Cutthroat Trout.

CAMP SPILLMAN

LOCATION AND DESCRIPTION

Start in Belfair. Take State Route 300 west for 3.6 miles. Turn right on Belfair Tahuya Road. Go 1.8 mile. Turn right on Elfendahl Pass Road. Go 2.6 miles. Turn left on Goat Ranch Road. Go 0.7 mile. Camp on right.

Washington State Department of Natural Resources 10 acre forest campground on the Tahuya River.

FACILITIES

6 campsites; 4 picnic table sites; fire grills; group amphitheatre; outhouse toilets; drinking water.

THINGS TO DO

Fishing; hiking; horseback riding; trailbike riding; picnicking; orv'g.

COMMENTS

Camp Spillman was formerly a camp for firefighters on the Tahuya Peninsula. A sign explaining the history of Camp Spillman and the only remaining evidence of the camp are by the river.

TWIN LAKES ACCESS

LOCATION AND DESCRIPTION

Eastside of the lake.

Washington State Department of Wildlife public access area to 12 acre Twin Lakes--51 feet of waterfront on .53 acres.

FACILITIES

1 lane boat launch ramp; 15 parking spaces; no drinking water.

THINGS TO DO

Fishing--Rainbow Trout.

COMMENTS

Fishing is fair for Rainbow Trout up to 9 inches.

TWIN (SPIDER) LAKES RECREATION CAMP

LOCATION AND DESCRIPTION

Start in Belfair. Take State Route 300 west for 3.6 miles. Turn right on Belfair Tahuya Road. Go 1.8 mile. Turn right on Elfendahl Pass Road. Go 2.6 mile. Turn left onto Goat Ranch Road and go 1.0 mile. Turn right onto Twin Lakes Road and go 1.0 miles to the camp.

Washington State Department of Natural Resources 12 acre campground on Twin Lakes. Twin Lakes is a beautiful lake in forest with view of Olympic Mountains.

FACILITIES

6 campsites with no hookups; tables; fire grills; parking; outhouse toilets; 3 picnic sites; no drinking water.

THINGS TO DO

Picnicking; hiking; fishing--Rainbow Trout.

TAHUYA RIVER HORSE CAMP

LOCATION AND DESCRIPTION

Start in Belfair. Take State Route 300 west for 3.6 miles. Turn right on Belfair Tahuya Road. Go 1.8 miles. Turn right on Elfendahl Pass Road. Go 2.7 miles. Turn left onto Goat Ranch Road which becomes So. Spillman and go 1.1 miles. Turn right and go .7 miles to camp.

Washington State Department of Natural Resources 12 acre horse camp on Tahuya River--beautiful flowing river with pools, gravel bars, and rapids.

FACILITIES

9 campsites with no hookups; tables and fire grills; horse pens made out of beautiful handhewn logs; 2 picnic sites; drinking water; outhouse toilets.

THINGS TO DO

Hiking; horseback riding; trailbike riding; picnicking; ORV'g.

COMMENTS

Special watering troughs for horses to drink out of and hitching posts will remind you of a western movie scene.

DEWATTO--PORT OF DEWATTO

LOCATION AND DESCRIPTION

From Holly take Dewatto Road W. south for 10.6 miles.

Dewatto is a small settlement on the south side of Dewatto Bay, a small shallow cove on the east shore of Hood Canal opposite Lilliwaup.

FACILITIES

Park.

THINGS TO DO

Boating; camping; picnicking.

COMMENTS

The Port of Dewatto Park on the Dewatto River is a short distance from the bay.

CLARA LAKE ACCESS

LOCATION AND DESCRIPTION

2 miles south of Dewatto on west side of lake.

Washington State Department of Wildlife public access area to 17 acre Clara Lake--200 feet of waterfront on 0.92 acres.

FACILITIES

1 lane boat launch; 30 parking spaces; no drinking water; fiberglass toilets.

THINGS TO DO

Fishing--Rainbow Trout.

COMMENTS

Fishing is fair to good for 7-9 inchers.

CADY LAKE ACCESS

LOCATION AND DESCRIPTION

2 miles southeast of Dewatto.

Washington State Department of Wildlife public access area to 15 acre Cady Lake--141 feet of waterfront on 1.57 acres.

FACILITIES

1 lane dirt boat launch ramp; 10 parking spaces; wood toilet.

THINGS TO DO

Fishing--Rainbow Trout, Cutthroat Trout.

COMMENTS

Fly fishing only. Receives a small plant of legal-size Rainbow Trout in spring besides normal crop of 7-13 inch Cutthroat Trout.

TEE LAKE ACCESS

LOCATION AND DESCRIPTION

From Dewatto 3 miles east. Area at north to northeast end of lake.

Washington State Department of Wildlife public access area to 38 acre Tee Lake--3.60 acres.

FACILITIES

1 lane dirt boat launch ramp; 20 parking spaces; wood toilet; no drinking water;

THINGS TO DO

Fishing--perch, bass, Rainbow Trout.

COMMENTS

Good perch and bass fishing, not so good for Rainbow Trout once the annual plants have been caught.

HOWELL LAKE RECREATION CAMP

LOCATION AND DESCRIPTION

Start in Belfair. Take State Route 300 west for 3.6 miles. Turn right on Belfair Tahuya Road. Go 4.1 miles, left 1.7 miles, camp on left.

Washington State Department of Natural Resources 20 acre campground on Howell Lake.

FACILITIES

6 campsites with no hookups (14 day limit); 3 picnic sites; tables and fire grills; hand boat launch; drinking water; outhouse toilets.

THINGS TO DO

Hiking; horseback riding; trailbike riding; fishing; ORV'g.

COMMENTS

Sign at outflow of lake explains how the Beaver is the only animal that can alter his environment, as shown by what he has done here.

HARVEY RENDSLAND STATE PARK

LOCATION AND DESCRIPTION

1.4 miles north of Tahuya by way of Belfair Tahuya Rd.

1,905 feet of shoreline on 8 acres incorporating one-half of Lake Rendsland, formerly Jiggs Lake. Presently park is undeveloped.

FACILITIES

None.

THINGS TO DO

Fishing--Largemouth Bass, perch, bullhead; picnicking; hiking.

COMMENTS

This property was willed to the Washington State Parks and Recreation Commission in 1971 at zero cost by Harvey Rendsland.

TAHUYA

LOCATION AND DESCRIPTION

From Dewatto take N.E. Dewatto Road 3.7 miles to N.E. Belfair Tahuya Road. Turn right and drive 4.3 miles. Turn right and drive .5 miles to Tahuya.

A small town on the north shore of The Great Bend.

FACILITIES

Commercial resort and marina with camping and boating facilities and supplies--boat rentals, propane, tackle, dock with floats, bait, moorage, annual spaces, boat launch ramp; cottages; ice; overnighters; RV spaces; country store; post office; lunch counter; gas; beauty salon.

THINGS TO DO

Boating; sightseeing.

COMMENTS

Tahuya Bay made a natural booming grounds--where the logs are kept in the water until towed to the mill-- and before there were roads to Tahuya a railroad line was built to bring logs out of the woods to the bay.

ALDRICH LAKE RECREATION CAMP

LOCATION AND DESCRIPTION

Start at town of Tahuya. Go north on Belfair-Tahuya Road 4.1 miles. Turn left on Dewatto Road for 2.1 miles. Turn left on Robbins Lake Road. Go 0.6 mile. Turn right. Go 0.7 mile. Turn right 0.1 mile to camp.

Washington State Department of Natural Resources 24 acre campground on 10 acre Aldrich Lake. This camp is unique with picturesque lake, campsites along edge of lake, scenic vista of Hood Canal and Olympics, and a trail that drops straight down bluff to canal.

FACILITIES

4 campsites (14 day limit in any 30 day period); 4 picnic sites; fire grills; tables; hand boat launch; outhouse toilets; drinking water; parking spaces.

THINGS TO DO

Fishing--Rainbow Trout; hiking; picnicking (day use only); camping.

COMMENTS

Boy Scout Camp Hahobas is right past entrance to Lake Aldrich.

ALDRICH LAKE ACCESS

LOCATION AND DESCRIPTION

Section 32, Township 23 N, Range 3 W.

Washington State Department of Wildlife public access area to Aldrich Lake--167 feet waterfront on .48 acres.

FACILITIES

1 lane boat launch ramp; 15 parking spaces.

THINGS TO DO

Fishing-- Rainbow Trout.

COMMENTS

Fishing is good for 8-10 inch Rainbow Trout.

ROBBINS LAKE RECREATION SITE

LOCATION AND DESCRIPTION

Start at town of Tahuya. Go north on Belfair Tahuya Road 4.1 miles. Turn left on Dewatto Road for 2.1 miles. Turn left on Robbins Lake Road. Go 0.6 mile. Turn left 0.9 mile to Robbins Lake. Turn right 0.2 mile to site.

Washington State Department of Natural Resources 1.06 acre campground on 17 acre Robbins Lake.

FACILITIES

3 picnic sites; tables; hand boat launch; fire grills; outhouse toilets; parking; no drinking water.

THINGS TO DO

Fishing--Rainbow Trout; picnicking.

COMMENTS

Good fishing for planted Rainbow Trout.

PORT OF ALLYN DOCK AND LAUNCH RAMP

LOCATION AND DESCRIPTION

4.4 miles southwest of Belfair on North Shore Road.
Dock with gangplank going down to moorage floats--
510 moorage float space footage (9 slips), fees.
1 lane boat launch ramp 1/10 of mile north of dock.

FACILITIES

Trash cans; parking; vault toilets.

THINGS TO DO

Boating.

MAGGIE LAKE ACCESS

LOCATION AND DESCRIPTION

2.2 miles northeast of Tahuya.
Washington State Department of Wildlife public access area to 25 acre Maggie Lake--96 feet of waterfront on .42 acres. Lake surrounded by houses.

FACILITIES

1 lane gravel boat launch ramp; 15 parking spaces; wood toilets.

THINGS TO DO

Fishing--Rainbow Trout.

COMMENTS

Fair action in spring from legal sized planted Rainbow Trout.

BELFAIR AREA PHEASANT RELEASE SITES

LOCATION AND DESCRIPTION

1) From Belfair turn left onto North Shore Road. Go 3.4 miles and turn right onto Belfair-Tahuya Road. Go 1.9 miles to Hurd Road. Turn left onto Hurd Road and take left gravel road opposite Macadam Road. (This is a total of 1.3 miles from Belfair-Tahuya Road) and release site is on right.

2) Coming from Gorst on old Belfair Highway turn right on Bear Creek-Holly Road. Just past Bear Creek Mini Mart, continue on Bear Creek-Holly Road 2 miles. Turn left on Mission Creek Youth Camp Road. Go 0.8 mile turn right. Go 0.2 mile. Turn right to release site.

FACILITIES

Limited parking.

THINGS TO DO

Ring-necked Pheasant hunting.

COMMENTS

The Washington State Department of Wildlife releases 2,440 Ring-necked Pheasants during the season with birds released primarily for Wednesday, weekend, and holiday hunting.

The birds are raised by The Washington State Department of Wildlife at The Lewis County Game Farm.

BELFAIR STATE PARK

LOCATION AND DESCRIPTION

2.9 miles west of Belfair on State Route 300.

62.98 acre Washington State Park near the southern end of Hood Canal noted for its saltwater tideflats. The park has over 3,000 feet of freshwater shoreline on Big Mission and Little Mission Creeks and over 2,100 feet of saltwater shoreline on Hood Canal.

FACILITIES

184 campsites, 47 with hookups (fees); dumpstation; tables; stoves; picnic shelter; primitive sites for bikers and hikers; restrooms with hot showers; day use area with a large field for baseball, soccer or football, unguarded swimming lagoon, picnic tables and stoves, horseshoe pit, volleyball area, and saltwater beach.

THINGS TO DO

Swimming; fishing; picnicking; camping; bicycling; birdwatching--Great Blue Heron, ducks, seagulls; beachcombing.

COMMENTS

In 1895 Big Mission and Little Mission Creeks were the site of a short lived gold rush.

ROESSEL ROAD SITE, UNION RIVER

LOCATION AND DESCRIPTION

Go to Belfair. Roessel Road. Section 29, Township 23 N, Range 1 W.

Washington State Department of Wildlife area--6,250 feet of waterfront tidelands and shorelands on north and south side of Union River on 53.21 acres.

FACILITIES

Hand boat launch area.

THINGS TO DO

Fishing--steelhead, trout; waterfowl hunting; bird watching.

COMMENTS

This site would be excellent for pheasants.

NORTH SHORE ROAD SITE, UNION RIVER

LOCATION AND DESCRIPTION

Go to Belfair. North Shore Road. Section 32, Township 23 N, Range 1 W.

Washington State Department of Wildlife area--1,848 feet of tidelands and shorelands on Union River on 8.6 acres.

FACILITIES

Hand boat launch area; 10 parking spaces.

THINGS TO DO

Fishing--steelhead and trout; waterfowl hunting; bird watching.

COMMENTS

This area of Hood Canal is one of the few remaining outstanding waterfowl areas left.

PANTHER LAKE ACCESS

LOCATION AND DESCRIPTION

From Belfair, 3.8 miles north and 3.6 miles northwest, south shore.

Washington State Department of Wildlife public access area to 100 acre Panther Lake--50 feet of waterfront on 3 acres. Lake has view of Olympics and Green Mountain to northeast (surrounded by cabins).

FACILITIES

1 lane gravel boat launch ramp; fiberglass toilets; 50 parking spaces; no drinking water.

THINGS TO DO

Fishing--Rainbow Trout.

COMMENTS

Fair fishing for Rainbow Trout under 12 inches.

GREEN MOUNTAIN RECREATION CAMP

LOCATION AND DESCRIPTION

Start on State Route 3 south of Silverdale. Go west on Newberry Hill Road for 3.1 miles. Turn left on Seabeck Highway 2.0 miles. Turn right on Holly Road. Go 4.0 miles. Turn left on Tahuya Lake Road. Go 0.9 mile. Turn left on Green Mountain Road (gravel). Go 2.7 miles to junction. Turn left 0.9 mile to camp or turn right 1.3 miles to 10 acre vista site.

Washington State Department of Natural Resources 23 acre camp.

FACILITIES

9 campsites; 2 picnic sites; horse facilities; outhouse toilets; drinking water. 2 picnic sites at vista.

THINGS TO DO

Horseback riding; hiking; ORV'g; trailbike riding.

COMMENTS

Drive to top of Green Mountain offers spectacular views of Seattle, Bremerton, Hood Canal, and the Olympic Mountains.

MISSION CREEK TRAILHEAD

LOCATION AND DESCRIPTION

Start in Belfair. Take State Route 300 west for 3.6 miles. Turn right on Belfair Tahuya Road. Go 1.1 miles. Trailhead on right.

Washington State Department of Natural Resources .49 acre forested area trailhead.

FACILITIES

None.

THINGS TO DO

Horseback riding; hiking; trailbikes.

TAHUYA 4 X 4 TRAILHEAD

LOCATION AND DESCRIPTION

Start in Belfair. Take State Route 300 west for 3.6 miles. Turn right on Belfair Tahuya Road. Go 1.8 miles and turn right on Elfendahl Pass Road. Go 2.3 miles. Trailhead on left.

Washington State Department of Natural Resources forested area trailhead for 4X4's.

FACILITIES

None.

THINGS TO DO

ORV'g.

COMMENTS

Tahuya 4X4 Trail was constructed by local volunteers from four wheel drive clubs.

TAHUYA RIVER

LOCATION AND DESCRIPTION

Start in Tahuya and drive northeast on the Tahuya River Road. Section 12, Township 22 N, Range 3 W, Subdivision SE 1/4, NE 1/4.

Washington State Department of Wildlife easement-- 25 foot strip of land bordering and extending along the north and south side of the Tahuya River for 700 feet.

FACILITIES

None.

THINGS TO DO

Fishing--trout, steelhead.

COMMENTS

Easement was granted March 25, 1954 by A. R. Cruikshank and his wife Caroline at no cost to the then Washington State Department of Game.

TOONERVILLE RECREATION CAMP

LOCATION AND DESCRIPTION

Start in Belfair. Take State Route 300 0.2 mile. Follow State Route 300 left for 3.3 miles. Turn right on Belfair-Tahuya Road. Go 0.6 mile. Turn right on Elfendahl Pass Road. Go. 2.6 miles on Elfendahl Pass Road. Go straight (through intersection with Goat Ranch Road) 3.3 miles. Camp on left.

Washington State Department of Natural Resources 5.7 acre forest campsite on beautiful clear flowing Tahuya River.

FACILITIES

4 campsites with no hookups; 2 picnic sites; tables and fire grills; outhouse toilets; picnic tables; no drinking water.

THINGS TO DO

Fishing; hiking; horseback riding; trailbike riding; ORV'g; picnicking.

COMMENTS

Trail along river.

TAHUYA RIVER

LOCATION AND DESCRIPTION

Start in Tahuya and drive northeast on the Tahuya River Road. Section 14, Township 22 N, Range 3 W, Subdivision NW 1/4, SW 1/4; Section 14 and 23, Township 22 N, Range 3 W, Subdivision NW 1/4, NE 1/4.

Washington State Department of Wildlife easement-- 3,700 feet of waterfront along east and west side of Tahuya River on 2.88 acres.

FACILITIES

Wood toilet.

THINGS TO DO

Fishing--trout, steelhead.

COMMENTS

The Tahuya River is known for its sea-run Cutthroat Trout.

REMOTE PLACES--BOAT AND FLOATPLANE ONLY

PORT GAMBLE BAY

LOCATION AND DESCRIPTION

Port Gamble Bay is 5 miles from the entrance to Hood Canal.

Port Gamble Bay is a small bay on the east side of Hood Canal. It is 2 miles long with a narrow entrance.

ANCHORAGE

Port Gamble Bay has excellent anchorage in 24 to 54 feet, muddy bottom.

THINGS TO DO

Boating; shellfish gathering--crabs (pot fishing); fishing.

COMMENTS

Port Gamble Bay has no shoreside facilities for boaters but the views are great and the anchorage is secure.

MISERY POINT FISHING REEF

LOCATION AND DESCRIPTION

NW of Seabeck on the east shore of Hood Canal.
Washington State Department of Fisheries fishing reef.

FACILITIES

None.

THINGS TO DO

Saltwater fishing.

SQUAMISH HARBOR

LOCATION AND DESCRIPTION

Squamish Harbor is an open bight just SW of Termination Point.

ANCHORAGE

You can anchor near the head of the harbor in about 6 fathoms in a muddy bottom.

THINGS TO DO

Boating; shellfish gathering.

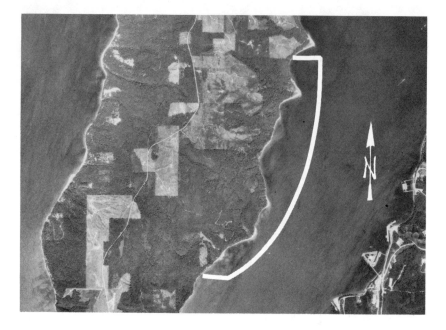

DNR BEACH 57B TOANDOS PENINSULA

LOCATION AND DESCRIPTION

11 nautical miles from Pt. Whitney, 14 nautical miles from Quilcene Bay, or 7 nautical miles from Seabeck. Beach below mean high water 10.0 feet.

The beach is 12,050 feet long. The upper beach is large cobble and the lower beach is sand.

FACILITIES

None.

THINGS TO DO

Shellfish gathering--Butter Clams, Iceland Cockles, Pacific Oysters, Littleneck Clams, Horse Clams.

COMMENTS

All surrounding beach and uplands are privately owned. Please do not trespass.

FISHERMAN HARBOR

LOCATION AND DESCRIPTION

Fisherman Harbor is a narrow cove on the south end of the Toandos Peninsula, just east of Oak Head. It has a constricted entrance which is only navigable at high water. A sandspit extends partly across the entrance from the west shore.

ANCHORAGE

Fisherman Harbor has secure anchorage in 2 fathoms in a muddy bottom.

THINGS TO DO

Boating; shellfish gathering--clams, oysters.

COMMENTS

Closeby the entrance to Fisherman Harbor are the Washington State Parks and Recreation Commission parks lands called Toandos Peninsula Tidelands--10,455 feet of waterfront.

DNR   BEACH   57   TABOOK   POINT,   TOANDOS PENINSULA

LOCATION AND DESCRIPTION

2 nautical miles from Point Whitney, 5 nautical miles from Quilcene Bay, or 7 nautical miles from Seabeck. Beach below mean high water 10.0 feet. The beach is 3,280 feet long.

The upper beach is broad and sandy and the lower beach is cobble gravel.

FACILITIES

None.

THINGS TO DO

Shellfish gathering--Pacific Oysters, Red Crab.

COMMENTS

All surrounding beach and uplands are privately owned. Please do not trespass.

DNR BEACH 40 ANDERSON COVE

LOCATION AND DESCRIPTION

9 nautical miles from Seabeck or 14 nautical miles from Potlatch. Beach below mean high water 10.8 feet. The beach is 2,145 feet long.

The south end of the beach is sand and mud covered with eelgrass and the remainder of the beach is cobble on upper beach, becoming sandier on the lower beach.

FACILITIES

None.

THINGS TO DO

Shellfish gathering--Butter Clams, Pacific Oysters, Blue Mussels, Littleneck Clams, Iceland Cockles, Dungeness Crabs.

COMMENTS

All surrounding beach and uplands are privately owned. Please do not trespass.

DNR BEACH 44A, 44B, 45 DEWATTO BAY

LOCATION AND DESCRIPTION

6 nautical miles from Potlatch, 8 nautical miles from Union, 17 nautical miles from Seabeck. South side of Dewatto Bay. Beach below mean high water 10.6 feet. Beach 44A is 514 feet long and Beach 44B is 713 feet long.

The upper beaches are gravel and the outer beaches are sand and mud.

FACILITIES

None.

THINGS TO DO

Shellfish gathering--Butter Clams, Pacific Oysters, Manila Clams, Horse Clams, Eastern Soft-shelled Clam, Blue Mussels, Red Crab, Dungeness Crab.

COMMENTS

All surrounding beaches and uplands are privately owned. Please do not trespass.

DNR BEACHES 46, 47, 48 HOOD CANAL

LOCATION AND DESCRIPTION

6-8 nautical miles from Potlatch, 8-10 nautical miles from Union, or 14--17 nautical miles from Seabeck. Beach below mean high water 10.8 feet. Beach 46 is 1,643 feet long, Beach 47 is 900 feet long, and Beach 48 is 9,072 feet long.

The beaches are cobble.

FACILITIES

None.

THINGS TO DO

Shellfish gathering--Pacific Oysters, Butter Clams, White Sand Macoma, Manila Clams, Littleneck Clams, sea cucumbers, Red Crab.

COMMENTS

All surrounding beach and uplands are privately owned. Please do not trespass.

DNR BEACH 50 TRITON COVE

LOCATION AND DESCRIPTION

7 nautical miles from Seabeck, 16 nautical miles from Hoodsport, 10 nautical miles from Pt. Whitney. Beach below mean high water 10.8 feet. The beach is 2,610 feet long.

The beach is cobble and small cobble and the southern 1/2 is sand.

FACILITIES

None.

THINGS TO DO

Shellfish gathering--Pacific Oysters, Littleneck Clams, Butter Clams, Geoducks, Dungeness Crab, Red Crab.

COMMENTS

All surrounding beach and uplands are privately owned. Please do not trespass.

DNR BEACH 55 JACKSON COVE

LOCATION AND DESCRIPTION

2 nautical miles from Pt. Whitney, 4 nautical miles from Quilcene Bay, or 7 nautical miles from Seabeck.

Beach below mean high water 10.8 feet. The mean high water line goes around the rock outcroppings, not over them. The beach is 2,791 feet long.

The south 1/2 of the beach is a rock ledge and the north 1/2 is gravel.

FACILITIES

None.

THINGS TO DO

Shellfish gathering--Pacific Oysters, Butter Clams, sea cucumbers, scallops.

COMMENTS

All surrounding beach and uplands are privately owned. Please do not trespass.

DNR BEACH 59 SHINE, SQUAMISH HARBOR

LOCATION AND DESCRIPTION

1/2 nautical mile from Shine or 2 nautical miles from Salsbury Point. Beach below mean high water 100 feet. The beach is 1,335 feet long.

The beach has a broad gravel upper beach and a flat sand lower beach.

FACILITIES

None.

THINGS TO DO

Shellfish gathering--Pacific Oysters, Littleneck Clams, Eastern Soft-shell Clams, Horse Clams, Iceland Cockles, Dungeness Crabs, Red Crabs.

COMMENTS

All surrounding beach and uplands are privately owned. Please do not trespass.

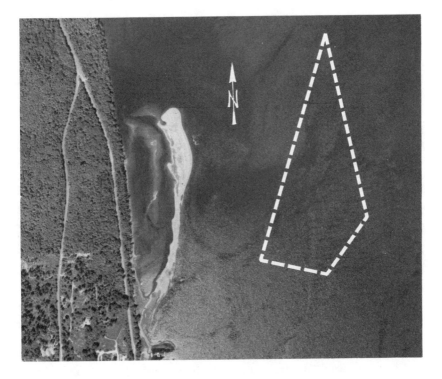

DNR BEACH 59A SHINE, CASE SHOAL

LOCATION AND DESCRIPTION

1 nautical mile from Shine or 2.5 nautical miles from Salsbury Pt.
Gravel beach.

FACILITIES

None.

THINGS TO DO

Shellfish gathering--below 2 feet--Butter Clams, Littleneck Clams, Horse Clams, maybe Geoducks.

COMMENTS

The entire exposed area is public ownership.

DABOB BAY

LOCATION AND DESCRIPTION

Dabob Bay is the largest inlet in Hood Canal and extends north for 9 miles. It is separated from the canal by the Toandos Peninsula. The entrance is between Tskutiko Point and Nlopash Point, just north of the mouth of the Dosewallips River.

The west shore of the bay is steep and imposing reaching an elevation of 2,600 feet in less than two miles from the shore.

ANCHORAGE

Jackson Cove.

THINGS TO DO

Boating; shellfish gathering--shrimp (pot fishing), clams, oysters.

COMMENTS

Jackson Cove is exposed to strong southerlies.

NELLITA

LOCATION AND DESCRIPTION

Nellita is south of Hood Point.
Beautiful cove with nice beach with little creeks flowing into canal.

FACILITIES

None.

THINGS TO DO

Explore ruins of foundation of old sawmill.

COMMENTS

Quaint old homes of Nellita's pioneer days are now converted to summer residences.

Chapter 9

HOOD CANAL KITCHEN
HOME RECIPES

I know you will enjoy the following recipes from the kitchens of the early residents of Hood Canal.

SALMON SOUFFLE

    1 cup salmon
    1 teaspoon salt
    1/8 teaspoon paprika
    2 teaspoons lemon juice
    3/4 cup soft bread crumbs
    3/4 cup milk
    3 eggs

Flake salmon. Add seasoning and lemon juice. Cook bread crumbs in milk 5 minutes. Add salmon. Cool. Beat egg yolks until lemon-colored and whites until stiff. Mix all together, turn into a buttered baking dish, set in a pan of hot water and bake in a moderate oven until firm.

Serve with cheese or Spanish sauce.

Spanish Sauce

    3 tablespoons butter
    3 tablespoons flour

1 1/2 cups milk
3 tablespoons pimiento, mashed to a paste
1/2 cup or more of cooked peas
Melt butter in saucepan. Add the flour and smooth to a paste. Add milk and stir until a smooth sauce is formed. Add pimiento and peas.

A ring mold may be used with cream peas in center of Salmon Souffle, using sauce in separate dish. Mary Hoogstins, Quilcene

SALMON SOUFFLE

2 tablespoons butter
2 tablespoons flour
1 cup milk
1/8 teaspoon salt
1 small onion, grated
1 cup or more of salmon
4 eggs
Make sauce of butter, flour, milk, salt, and grated onion. Add salmon (flaked, skinned, and boned). Remove from fire, add well-beaten egg yolks. Cool, fold in egg whites beaten stiff. Bake in buttered baking dish, set in pan of hot water in 325 degree oven for 1 hour. Serve with hollandaise sauce. (Mrs. Arthur B. Langlie) Evelyn Baker Langlie, Olympia

SALMON SOUFFLE

3 tablespoons butter
1/4 cup flour
1/2 teaspoon salt
Dash of pepper
Liquid drained from salmon plus evaporated milk to make 3/4 cup
1 cup salmon
3 eggs, separated
1/4 teaspoon baking powder
Melt butter in saucepan, add flour, salt and pepper. Stir to blend well. Add milk and salmon liquid. Cook until quite thick, stirring constantly. Add salmon and cool a little. Add beaten egg yolks and baking powder. Stir only enough to blend, fold in stiffly-beaten egg

whites. Turn into well-greased baking dish. Bake at 300 degrees for 45 minutes. Patricia Rihtarich

SALMON LOAF

- 2 egg yolks
- 1 cup scalded milk
- 1 cup dry bread crumbs
- 1 teaspoon onion juice
- 1 teaspoon lemon juice
- 1 teaspoon salt
- 1 can salmon
- 2 egg whites (stiffly beaten)

Pour milk over bread crumbs and let soak. Mix other ingredients with milk and crumb mixture. Fold in egg whites last. Put in greased casserole and bake in 350 degree oven 45 minutes. Marjorie Morse Coffland

SALMON PEPPERED, QUILCENE STYLE

- 4 tablespoons flour
- 4 tablespoons butter
- 1 1/2 cups milk
- 1/2 cup sharp cheese
- 6 large peppers
- 2 cups salmon flaked
- 2 cups whole kernel corn

Salt and pepper to taste
Dash of garlic or onion salt

Cut top from peppers, remove seeds and parboil for 3 minutes. Drain. Place in baking dish and add following mixture: Melt butter and add flour and brown, and add milk to make white sauce. Stir in cheese until melted, season with salt and pepper. Add salmon and corn. Fill peppers with salmon mixture and bake in hot oven about 20 minutes. Dick Danielsen

BROILED SALMON (SALMON, TROUT)

For fishes that are fat, such as chinook and the chum, broiling is one of the most satisfactory cooking methods. Although some may prefer to leave the skin on the fish, it is a common practice to skin and fillet them. Cut into 1/2 pound portions and place under broiler that has been pre-heated to a temperature of 400 degrees F. Brush several times with butter, bacon drippings, or other fat while cooking and season with salt and pepper. To test for doneness, insert knife in the thickest point. The knife point will enter easily if fish is well done. Color should be pink instead of red. For an ordinary fillet 1 inch thick, 8 to 10 minutes cooking time is usually sufficient, if the cut is turned once.

BOUILLABAISE A LA BRINNON

A Bouillabaise is a soup of which the stock is made of fish meat and not of beef. It originates from the shores of the Mediterranean Sea where every locality has its own brand of Bouillabaise. The three essentials of the Bouillabaise are: (1) the stock, (2) the filling, and (3) the flavoring. This explains why there are so many varieties of Bouillabaise, for by varying the kind of fish employed in the stock, or the material employed in the filling, or the herbs used in the flavoring you can obtain a new Bouillabaise. For instance, in North Africa the favorite fish used in the soup is gray mullet. The filling is composed of millet to which is added chopped urchin meat and the flavoring pungent herbs from the dry Atlas Mountains. Around the Port of Bone in Algeria the soup often contains pieces of lamb kidney. Around Marseille the stock is made from strong-tasting red mullet, the filling is stewed fish and lobster added to potatoes, oil and oats. The soup is strongly flavored with garlic and saffron. The fact is that a Bouillabaise depends on the materials easily available.

The Brinnon Bouillabaise has as a base one or more of the following fish: flounder, rock cod, ling cod, bull-head, perch, in fact it can be made of any non-oily fish. Never, never use an oily fish such as a salmon or herring or sable fish to make this soup. If care is taken to eliminate every trace of liver or innards you can use rock cod heads, ling cod heads, but flounder heads are too oily. The body of the Brinnon Bouillabaise is com-posed of potatoes, onions, barley, with Wesson or any cooking oil and flour. The soup is flavored with salt, celery seed and curry powder and can be rounded out with a 1/2 glass of sherry.

A variant of the Brinnon soup is the Quilcene Bouillabaise, the filling of which includes chopped oysters, chopped clams and crab meat.

Two-Quart Recipe:

Stock: Liquid from 2 pounds cleaned fish (use skin and bone) or more.

Filling:

1 large potato, cubed
1 large onion chopped
1 cup barley
1 cup flour
3/4 cup cooking oil

Flavoring:

1 teaspoon celery seed
1 teaspoon salt according to taste
1/2 teaspoon curry powder
Small glass of sherry

Process: Boil fish in about 2 1/2 quarts water, to allow for evaporation, for about 1/2 hour or more. Separate stock from fish by pouring into strainer. (The frugal French save the cooked fish to add to the soup, but it is so tasteless it is better for the chickens.)

Put soup in large kettle and add the potato, the onion and the barley, and cook until tender. Mix flour and oil thoroughly and add to stock. Cook and add all flavoring except sherry which should be added just before the soup is ready to serve. The consistency of soup should be about that of Scotch Broth but not as thick as that of pea soup. This soup is improved with the addition of crab, shrimp or oysters, but they are not essential. If you have any non-oily cooked fish meat you can add it to the filling just before serving. Don't overcook these additional ingredients. Major M.J. Hopkins, Brinnon, Wash.

BAKED OYSTERS

Cover bottom of buttered baking dish with a layer of oysters. Season with paprika and sprinkle a pinch of horseradish over each one.

To 1/2 cup fresh bread crumbs add 2 tablespoons grated Parmesan cheese and 2 tablespoons grated Swiss cheese. Mix thoroughly and cover the oysters with prepared crumbs. Dot with butter and bake in a moderate oven until nicely browned.

Garnish with sprigs of parsley and quartered lemon.

Repeat above for a second layer, but never cook 3 layers as middle layer will be underdone while bottom and top will be overdone. Mrs. Maurice J. Hopkins, Brinnon

BAKED OYSTERS

Put fresh oysters in clean baking shells and pour sauce over them topping with strips of bacon.

Sauce:

Home-made chili or catsup base with chopped green peppers, Worcestershire sauce and a bit of chopped onion added to taste. Bake 10 minutes in a 400 degree oven. Delicious served with baked potatoes on the half shell. Florence L. Jespersen

HILLS' HALF ACRE--OYSTERS ROCKEFELLER

Cut our Canal oysters in three or four pieces. Put generous amount in large oyster shell, or layer in casserole. Salt, pepper. Add part of a butter mixture, which includes melted butter, onion juice, chopped parsley, a little dry mustard and lemon juice to taste. Next add a layer of browned bacon bits, then pureed spinach (we use canned baby-food spinach for this). Then add cracker crumbs and the remaining butter. Bake in oven 450 to 500 degrees for 12 to 15 minutes or until plump. Frances Hill

OYSTER POKIE

Use large oysters, have them freshly opened, retaining them in their shells. Make a sauce of tomato catsup, minced onion, and a pinch of thyme. Have small slices of bacon cut into small bits. Lay bacon bits on top of oysters and spoon sauce on top. Place to brown under grill for 4 minutes, or until bacon is browned and edges of oysters begin to curl. Serve immediately. Mrs. Warren Stewart, Lilliwaup, Wash.

QUILCENE OYSTER PIE

Line a pudding dish with a pastry made as follows:
1 pint flour, sifted
1 teaspoon baking powder
Lard, size of an egg
A little salt
Use 1 quart oysters. Place in dish enough to cover bottom. Over this put salt and pepper, bits of parsley and thyme, pieces of butter, and 1 hard-boiled egg cut in pieces. Over this lay bits of dough rolled thin. Repeat this, beginning with another layer of oysters. Add to the whole enough of the liquor and some milk to almost cover it. Put on top a layer of pastry and bake in a moderate oven for about 1 hour. Dick Danielsen

PAN-BAKED OYSTERS

Salt and beat 1 egg, roll the oysters in crumb or cracker meal, dip in egg, and into crumbs again. Place in shallow pan with plenty of butter. Bake in medium-hot oven. Mrs. Florence Oslund

OYSTER RAMEKIN

8 ounces macaroni
12 medium oysters
1 7-ounce can tuna fish
1/4 pound grated cheese
1 1/2 cups mushroom sauce or a 16-ounce can mushroom soup, diluted with 1/2 cup oyster liquor, plus seasoning given in sauce recipe
Cook macaroni, simmer oysters in enough water to cover. Drain and chop. Save oyster liquor for sauce. Add tuna fish, oysters, cheese, to mushroom sauce. Heat through, about 10 minutes, pour over macaroni, heat 5 minutes more and serve in ramekins.
Mushroom sauce for above:

3 tablespoons butter in skillet, sautee chopped mushrooms

Remove mushrooms, and add:

3 tablespoons flour

1 cup hot milk, added slowly with 1/2 cup oyster liquor

1 teaspoon each Worcestershire sauce, curry poweder, oinion salt, dash of pepper and 2 tablespoons catsup Ann Ruedy

OYSTERS EN CASSEROLE

1 pint oysters cut to bite size

1/2 cup cracker or bread crumbs

1 egg

About 2 cups thin white sauce

Make white sauce, cool, beat in egg. Butter baking dish, sprinkle thin layer crumbs on bottom, put in 1/4 oysters, few more crumbs, some sauce, repeat till all are used, cover top with crumbs, dot with butter, sprinkle with paprika. Bake quickly till brown. Chopped pimiento or green pepper may be added if desired. Crab meat is very good served this way. Jane Nordean

OYSTER CASSEROLE

1 cup chopped mushrooms

8 to 10 small whole mushrooms

1/2 cup butter

1 cup cracker crumbs

1 1/2 pints oysters

1 cup milk

1/2 cup light cream

Paprika seasoning

Saute all mushrooms in 2 tablespoons butter for 2 minutes. Line a casserole with 1/2 the crumbs, add a layer of chopped mushrooms and dot with 1 tablespoon butter. Add another layer of crumbs, then oysters and remaining chopped mushrooms, then a final layer of crumbs. Pour milk and cream and 5 tablespoons melted butter over the top. Set casserole in a pan of water and bake in moderate oven, 375 degrees for 25 minutes. Stand whole mushrooms upright in crumbs, sprinkle with paprika. Place in moderate broiler, heat about 5 minutes. Serves 6. Mrs. Grace Kline

SCALLOPED OYSTERS AND MACARONI

1 cup macaroni
2 cups oysters
1/2 cup bread crumbs
1/4 cup grated cheese
2 tablespoons butter
1 cup milk
Salt and pepper to season

Cook macaroni in boiling salted water. Drain. Rinse with cold water. Fill well-oiled baking dish with alternate layers of macaroni and oysters. Add milk. Dot each layer with butter, add seasonings. Cover top with bread crumbs. Sprinkle with grated cheese. Bake in moderate oven 375 degrees for about 40 minutes. Serves 6 to 8. Helen L. Ward

SCALLOPED OYSTERS

1 pint fresh oysters, washed carefully
10 to 12 soda crackers
1/2 pint cream or rich top milk
A little butter and black pepper

Take baking dish and crumble a layer of crackers, pour in oysters, then the remaining crackers real fine, pour cream over and place dots of butter on top and a little black pepper. Bake 30 minutes or until oysters are done. Mrs. Cox

BARBECUED OYSTER LOAF

1 1/2 pounds chopped oysters
1/4 cup chopped onion
1 1/2 teaspoons salt
1/8 teaspoon pepper
1 teaspoon Worcestershire sauce
1 1/2 cups soft bread crumbs
1/2 cup tomato juice
2 slices bacon
1/2 cup catsup or chili sauce

Combine all ingredients except catsup or chili sauce. Pack into greased loaf pan. Baste with catsup or chili sauce. Bake at 300 degrees for 1 hour. Martha L. Mulkey

OYSTERS PORT AND STARBOARD

1 cup thick cream sauce
1 pint oysters
1/2 cup chopped cooked mushrooms
1 pimento, chopped
1 tablespoon chopped parsley
1 egg hard boiled, chopped
1/4 teaspoon Worcestershire sauce
Salt and pepper to taste
Cracker crumbs

Cook oysters in liquor until edges curl, about 5 minutes. Strain off, cool and chop in pieces, not too small. Make 1 cup thick cream sauce and add it to oysters, mushrooms, pimento, parsley, egg and seasonings. Put into greased quahaug shells and sprinkle with crumbs. Put shells on cookie sheet and bake 425 degrees for 10 minutes. Jane Nordean

OYSTER POTATO SURPRISE

1 pint hot seasoned mashed potatoes
1 beaten egg
1 teaspoon minced onion
18 oysters well drained

Blend potatoes, beaten egg and minced onion into flat cakes. Make pocket in potato cake and insert 3 drained oysters. Replace potato covering. Place cakes on well-greased glass baking pan and bake in moderate oven until brown. Serve with tomato or chili sauce thinned with olive oil. Mrs. Warren Stewart, Lilliwaup, Wash.

QUILCENE PERFECT OYSTER STEW

1 quart oysters solid pack and grade B or C, creamy plump in appearance. Big grade A oysters will not do.
1 quart and 1 cup grade A whole milk

4 tablespoons butter, not margarine
1 tablespoon salt
1 teaspoon pepper

Put oysters in flat enamel pan. Cover with cold water, add salt, pepper and butter. Gently boil till tender enough to pierce easily with fork, about 20 minutes.

Place milk in top of double boiler, heat to scalding (boiling point), place over hot water at once, as loss of raw taste is desired. Over-cooking at high heat causes scum and flavor loss.

To serve: It is important never to combine milk and oysters anywhere but in the pre-heated soup bowls. Then each individual's preference may have the amount of oysters, liquor, or milk accordingly.   To accompany, cabbage slaw is nice and plenty of hot coffee a must.
Mrs. Frank H. Beck

OYSTER SUPREME

Saute in 4 tablespoons shortening:
1/2 cup chopped onions
1 clove chopped garlic
1/4 cup chopped green pepper
Add, and cook slowly for 30 minutes:
2 cups canned tomatoes
4 cups water
2 1/2 teaspoons salt
Dash cayenne pepper
1/8 teaspoons chili pepper
1 cup uncooked rice

Add 1 pint oysters, cut to bite size. Heat thoroughly and serve with garlic bread.

JOSIE PETERSON'S OYSTER CHOWDER

Many people make clam chowder, but we had never thought of making oyster chowder until the suggestion came from Mrs. Josie Peterson, our neighbor on Indian Beach. She makes it exactly like clam chowder, excepting for using our cut-up oysters instead of clams. She uses the Pacific Coast Clam Chowder recipe, which calls for the following to serve six to eight people:
3 large potatoes, diced

1 onion, chopped
Chopped celery and parsley or chives to taste
3 or 4 slices of bacon, diced and browned
1 can evaporated milk
Boil the potatoes and celery in quart of water. Onions can be cooked with potatoes or browned with bacon. Do not pour off water. Add clams or oysters to cooked potatoes, bring to boil for a couple of minutes, stir in milk, bacon bits, parsley or chives. Remove from fire. This can be prepared ahead, with the exception of the milk, which can be added and brought to boil before serving. Frances Hill

OYSTER PEPPER PAN ROAST

4 teaspoons butter
1 cup oysters
1 cup catsup
1/4 cup chopped green peppers
1/4 cup celery
Season with salt and pepper and fry celery and peppers in butter. Add oysters and cook until edges curl. Mrs. E.R. McDonald

OYSTER DELIGHT

1 dozen oysters
1 tablespoon butter or margarine
Juice of 1/2 lemon
1 egg yolk and 1 teaspoon flour
Minced parsley
Salt to taste
1/2 cup light cream
Scald the oysters in their own liquor. Salt and remove the oysters. Add to the liquor the butter, lemon juice, cream and flour. While the sauce is simmering beat the egg yolk, add and allow to simmer until thickened. Place oysters and cubed toast on a hot dish and pour sauce over them. Sprinkle with parsley and serve at once. Serve 4. Mrs. Warren Stewart, Lilliwaup, Wash.

QUILCENE OYSTER CLUB SANDWICH

1 pint oysters
6-12 slices bacon
1/2 cup flour
1/2 teaspoon salt
1/8 teaspoon pepper
12 lettuce leaves
12 slices tomato
1 tablespoon horseradish
1/2 cup mayonnaise
18 slices thin crisp butter toast

Fry bacon until crisp. Drain on absorbent paper. Roll oyster in flour seasoned with salt and pepper. Fry in bacon fat. When brown on one side turn and brown on the other side. Cook about 5 minutes. Drain. If large oysters, slice each into halves lengthwise. Arrange lettuce, oysters, bacon, tomatoes between 3 slices of bread. Dress with mayonnaise mixed with horseradish. Fasten with toothpicks at center of each side, then cut the sandwich into halves diagonally, using sharp knife. Dick Danielsen

OYSTER FRICASSE

Drain 1 quart of oysters, reserve liquor and heat to boiling point. Wash oysters, add to liquor, and cook until plump and the gills curl, then remove and skim. Strain well. Add enough milk to make 2 cups. Melt 4 tablespoons butter, add 4 tablespoons flour and gradually the hot liquid. Cook until thickened, add a few grains of cayenne, 1/2 teaspoon salt, 2 teaspoons chopped parsley. Pour this over 2 eggs slightly beaten. Add oysters. Cook 1 minute. Serve in a border of mashed potatoes. Louis Pennini, Brinnon

OYSTER STUFFING

2 cups dry bread crumbs (no crust)
1 1/2 cups cracker crumbs
2 teaspoons salt
Paprika
3/4 cup melted butter

1/2 teaspoon pepper
1 1/2 pints oysters, cleaned and muscle removed
Mix all ingredients, toss with fork. Heat oysters in own liquid, drain before using. Mrs. Richard Corey

GOEDUCK OR CLAM CHOWDER

2 large potatoes
1 large onion
1/2 cup ham or bacon
1/8 cup celery
1 1/2 cups goeduck or clams

Grind all ingredients through medium food grinder, cover with water and cook until potatoes are tender. If you wish to serve with milk heat milk and add after chowder is cooked, if not add more water and a little more butter and serve. Salt and pepper to taste. Care must be taken not to burn. Mrs. Cox

FRIED CLAMS

Flour clams by shaking them in a paper bag with flour, salt, and pepper. Brown quickly on top of stove, then place them in a roaster with a clove of garlic and a small onion. Let them steam in a slow oven, 250 degrees, for 2 hours. Mrs. Florence Oslund

CLAM CHOWDER

1 gallon clams in shells

Steam. Remove and discard contents of stomach and black head. Grind in food chopper with 1 large potato and 1 large onion. Boil in nectar. Cube a 4-inch square of salt pork in skillet, add dash of pepper and add to clam chowder. Cook slowly. Mrs. Tooker

CLAMBERGERS

1 pint minced clams
2 well-beaten eggs
1 large onion, minced
Flour to hold together
Salt
Fry in hot fat.   Johnny Boyce

CLAM "U" KNOW

1 pint clams, chopped fine
1 egg well beaten
1 cup cracker crumbs
1 teaspoon salt
1/4 teaspoon pepper
1 teaspoon finely chopped onion (optional)

Combine ingredients in order given and mix well. Form in round cakes and fry in hot fat, about 1 inch deep. Drain and serve piping hot on hot platter. This is a favorite way of cooking clams for a large gathering. Mrs. Warren Stewart, Lilliwaup, Wash.

CLAM OMELET

Pour nectar from 1 can of clams into small sauce pan. Add equal amount of hot water, let simmer. To the clams add 3 well-beaten eggs, fry in a skillet in bacon grease about 2 or 3 minutes until brown on bottom, turn and bake until brown again. Serve on lettuce leaf with slices of ripe tomatoes and olives (if liked) or serve with a glass of tomato juice. Serve nectar in small glasses, add pinch of finely-cut parsley and a small piece of butter to each glass. Serve hot. With the omelet this makes a tasty luncheon dish. One can serves 3 persons. Mrs. Paul Schechert

CREAMED CLAMS IN SHELLS

1 tablespoon butter
2 tablespoons flour

Add juice from 1 can of clams and 1/2 cup cream, stir until smooth. Add the minced clams, a dash of salt, pepper and Worcestershire sauce.

Put in shells (deep cockle clam shells are nice) sprinkled with buttered bread crumbs on top and place under broiler to brown slightly. Larger servings in the shells can make the main dish for luncheons, with salad, hot rolls, etc. It is very nice as it does not cool off too quickly.

It can be made with raw minced clams direct from the beach to the oven, so to speak. Mrs. Bertha Sund, Brinnon

CREAMED CLAMS AS ENTREE

    1 can minced white clams
    4 cups thick white sauce
    3 hard-boiled eggs

Make white sauce, cool, beat in egg. Butter baking dish, sprinkle thin to boiling point, remove from heat and add eggs. Serve on toast. Mrs. Cox

SCALLOPED POTATOES AND CLAMS

Chop 3/4 pound bacon, brown in frying pan, remove bacon, pour off about half the grease, cut up 4 or 5 stems of celery, 2 onions, fry until transparent but not brown. Grind clams. Put layer of clams in casserole, then a layer of sliced potatoes, then a layer of bacon and celery. Sprinkle in a little flour. Fill casserole, leaving potatoes on top. Add milk until 1/3 of the dish is full. Bake in 350 degree oven for 1 hour, or until potatoes are done.

GOEDUCK OR CLAM LOAF

    2 cups ground goeduck or clams
    2/3 cup sweet milk
    1/2 teaspoon salt, and a dash of pepper
    1 cup medium fine ground cracker crumbs
    2 eggs well beaten

Mix all above ingredients together and put into a well-greased baking dish or casserole. Dot top with butter and crackers. Bake in moderate oven at 350 degrees for one hour. Mrs. Kenneth D. Hart

CLAM LOAF

    1 can minced clams
    1 small onion, minced
    1/2 pound sausage
    1 cup cracker crumbs

2 eggs, beaten

Salt and pepper to taste

Mix all ingredients and bake in moderate oven 40 minutes. Dick Danielsen

FRIED RAZOR CLAMS

Salt clams well, then shake in paper sack, which contains flour. Dip in beaten egg, then in rolled crackers. Fry in very hot deep fat only 1 1/2 to 2 minutes to each side. Long frying toughens clams. Elva Horn

SHRIMP 'N CHIPS

Beat 1 egg, 3 tablespoons milk, pinch salt, 2 tablespoons flour, 1/2 teaspoon baking powder (thin batter). Put into it enough shrimp for desired servings. Pick up shrimp out of the batter with a fork, drop into hot fat to brown quickly, serve on hot buttered toast, with white or cheese sauce if desired. Serves 4 to 6. Jane Nordean

SHRIMP IN SAUCE

1 pint peeled shrimp, fresh or canned

4 tablespoons butter

1 teaspoon minced onion

1 teaspoon chili powder

4 tablespoons flour

2 cups milk

2 tablespoons minced parsley

1/4 cup tomato catsup

Heat the butter and minced onion, add the shrimp and brown. Stir in the flour, chili powder and the milk. Cook from 8 to 10 minutes. Add catsup and parsley and steam several minutes before serving hot on buttered toast. Mrs. Jack Colegrove

SAUCE FOR FRENCH FRIED SHRIMP

1 cup Miracle Whip, or mayonnaise

1 onion chopped (not too fine)

Add catsup to color. May be used over crab or red snapper. Gladys Howell

FRESH SHRIMP CHOWDER

    2 pounds fresh shrimp
    1 cup chopped celery
    1 cup diced raw potatoes
    1 medium-sized carrot (diced)
    1 large onion, minced
    Thyme, salt and pepper to taste
Boil, clean and strain shrimp, putting liquid aside. Saute vegetables in 2 tablespoons of butter, or a little salt pork may be added if desired. Do not brown. Add 4 cups of water and simmer 1/2 hour. To this add the shrimp liquid and the shrimps which have been cut into quarter pieces. More water may be added to this if it appears too thick. Allow to simmer for 1/2 hour additional, add thyme, pepper and it is ready to serve. Will serve 6 persons. Dick Danielsen

SHRIMP FRITTERS

    2 cups cooked shrimp
    1 egg, beaten
    1 small onion
    Salt and pepper to taste
Grind shrimp and onion. Combine with egg and seasonings. Drop by spoonfuls in hot shortening. Brown thoroughly. Serve immediately. Dick Danielsen

FISH CHOWDER

Use red snapper or any white fresh fish. Place in a deep iron skillet a layer of finely-cut bacon, on top of that a layer of fish. Above that a layer of thinly-sliced raw Irish potatoes and a layer of thinly-sliced onion. Lastly, a layer of soda cracker crumbs dotted with butter.

Repeat until pot is filled. Add water half way to the height of the cooking utensil. Cover and simmer until onions and potatoes are tender. The liquid must cook entirely away so that the bottom layer becomes well-browned.

Add cream to cover, heat to boiling and serve immediately. Mrs. T.B. Balch, Brinnon

CLAM BAKE

Dig a pit one foot deep by three feet wide (6-8 people's serving). Line pit with large rocks along bottom and sides. Build fire on rocks to heat hot and thoroughly. Build fire of dry wood, not green or pitchy woods, using hardwood, such as iron-wood, hazel, vinemaple, or yew-wood. Clean rocks thoroughly of all coats and foreign matter before putting in clams. Clams should be dug the day before and left in fresh water overnight. A handful of cornmeal to a bucket will help rid them of their sand. Put clams on rocks and cover completely with clean sacks or seaweed that is clean. Allow clams to remain about twenty minutes in "oven." Inspect at the end of this time, and if open, they are ready. If not, recover until they open. Large clean clam shells can hold butter, melted by the fire for dipping the clams prior to eating.

PHEASANT, SCOTTISH

Hang the pheasant by the heels in the game room (or cold pantry) for 10 days to 2 weeks. Feathers will pull off easily. Clean. Stuff with your favorite poultry stuffing. Brown in grease, preferably bacon drippings. Roast in pan, covering bird with oven paper, for 1/2 hour. Then remove paper and brown for 20 minutes or more, depending on your oven.

Roast pheasant dry. Don't put water in your roaster unless you want steamed pheasant. The bird is juicy enough; preserve its own rare flavor.

Take brown bread or hard toast, crumble it, stir crumbs in hot bacon grease, crisp in frying pan or oven, and serve as crackers with the bird. Mrs. James Ramsay

PHEASANTS

A small amount of flour, salt, pepper, butter. Clean breast, legs, wash well and dry, roll in flour, salt and pepper. Fry in butter until light brown. Then put in roasting pan. Make thin sauce of butter, flour, cream. Pour over bird. Roast until tender. Add more cream if necessary. Washington Game Department Official

ROAST PHEASANT WITH DRESSING

2 pheasants
Butter
Dry bread
Marjoram
Salt
Thyme
Pepper
Sweet basil
1 egg
Flour
1 slice ham
1 small pheasant or parts of pheasant
1/4 cup white wine
1/4 cup button mushroom

Remove all meat from 1 small pheasant or usable pieces from badly-shot birds and broil for 4 minutes along with a slice of good Virginia ham. Mince the broiled pheasant meat, dice ham and add 1/4 cup button mushrooms. Season generously with salt, pepper, and pinch each of thyme, marjoram and sweet basil. (Some good poultry seasoning may be used.) Saute this stuffing for 5 minutes in hot butter, draw aside and add 1 cup dry coarse bread crumbs, bind with 1 beaten egg and cold water if necessary. Dredge with a bit of flour and stuff birds.

Then roast in a buttered ovenware dish at 350 degrees until tender, 2 1/2 to 3 1/2 hours depending on size and age of birds. Baste with plenty of melted butter mixed with white wine. Make gravy from the cooking juices. Taken from the South Dakota Pheasant Hunting Guide

QUAIL AND BISCUITS

6 quail (any number)

Pluck; disjoin backbone. Flour and place in buttered bake pan. Add seasoning including a clove of garlic chopped. Cover with hot water. Place in oven, 350 degrees for 2 to 2 1/2 hours or until water has nearly all boiled away.

Again add boiling water in 1/2 the previous amount. Put in oven until quail are tender. Cover entire dish with baking powder biscuits. Replace in 450 degree oven until done. A Game Protector's Wife

WILD BLACKBERRY PIE

Use fresh or frozen berries, adding sugar to taste. About 3 cups of berries is sufficient for 1 pie. Add an envelope of plain gelatin to the berries and thoroughly mix. Use a graham cracker crust and chill until served. Patricia Campbell, Port Ludlow

Chapter 10

MEMORIES OF EARLY PIONEERS

History will come alive as you read the remembrances of these early Hood Canal pioneers.

MEMORIES OF A HAZEL POINT PIONEER--LEO J WOOD

My family settled on the Toandos (Coyle) peninsula in Jefferson County on the first day of May 1889. At that time I was a babe in arms. Traveling overland from Kansas the family group included my parents, John F. and Alice Eva (Todd) Wood, my uncle James Bradford Wood, his wife and my paternal grandparents. At Hazel Point members of my family filed on homesteads.

My mind goes back to those early days. The waters of Hood Canal, the deep, dark forests, the wild animals that roamed the woods--cougars, bobcats, bear and deer, and the struggles of men and women in a new country-- all of these things made a deep impression upon me. There were Indians, too. The ones who lived near Coyle were the Siwash. Others, such as the Clallams, Quilcenes and Skohomish, came up the Canal every fall. Hazel Point was one of their stopping places. They traveled in big cedar canoes. The older Indians behaved very well but the younger ones were ornery, disagreeable and mean. I knew the Prince of Wales and his wife. The Prince was the son of the Duke of York or Chetzemoka. In the late twenties or early thirties they lived at Coyle on Fisherman's Harbor.

The school I attended was built of logs. The only boughten piece of furniture in that school was the teacher's chair. Seats and desk and even the blackboard were homemade. There were about thirty-five or forty children going to that one-room school. The teacher's name was William Mitchell, who taught all the grades. From our home on the Canal I walked a mile to school.

Once I had photographs of the school and school children. When my mother died my father turned everything over to my sister, Mrs. Harry Eaton, who was living at Coyle. When my sister died, my niece, Mrs. John Bergeson of Coyle took the pictures. They went up in flames when fire destroyed the house.

As a youngster I walked along the tidelands, stopping occasionally at a big rock, located in front of our home. Below the center of the rock was a big hole, filled with sea water. One day, while wading in this pool, a crab reached out, grabbed me by the big toe and held on. I struggled but couldn't get loose. The tide was coming in fast. Hearing my cries, my father saved me by breaking the crab's pincers. He said it was the biggest Dungeness crab he had ever seen.

Working with my father, I learned all about logging. An axe, saw and adz were the basic tools. My dad made a living cutting shingles by hand and taking them in a rowboat to Port Gamble, where he sold them for a dollar a thousand. Going along with my dad, we usually arrived at Port Gamble about daylight. My dad would take me into the cookhouse, where Chinese cooks took care of me. Those trips to Port Gamble were one of the highlights of my boyhood.

Logging is remindful of oxen and skid roads. They go together. There were no wharves in those days. Oxen would be driven aboard steamboats and when the boats reached a designated point, the oxen would be pushed overboard by deck hands. Bawling and spurting water the oxen reached shore. I remember a logger named Valentine. He had eight oxen and I can recall the names of four of them. One pair responded to the names of Buck and Bawley and the other to Dick and Dine.

My dad and Uncle Jim cut telephone poles and logged them into the canal. Loggers took out the choicest old growth Douglas fir. They didn't bother with any of the small stuff. Many of the logs were from four to eight feet in diameter. The biggest ever felled measured ten feet eight inches in diameter; that was called the old growth. It was clear timber and it was soft; the harder tree is found in the second growth areas. The big lumber mills were at Port Ludlow, Port Gamble and Fort Blakely.

My dad occasionally took me to Quilcene. That is where I saw my first train--the old Port Townsend Southern. At Port Gamble and Port Ludlow I saw many Chinese working on ships, loading lumber. At Dabob lived my Uncle Lashua Moore, grandfather of Milo Moore, my second cousin, who was formerly fish commissioner.

I was a timber faller in this district twenty-five years. Also I have been in the Wildlife service of the government, spending twelve years in the Bristol Bay district, Alaska. Having reached the age of 77 in 1966 I have settled down to enjoy retirement in Port Townsend. Of the original members of the Wood families who crossed the plains in 1889, only three are left. There is my cousin Clarence Wood in Dabob, his sister Flora Lathrop of Paso Robles, California, and myself.

Hazel Point

MEMORIES OF A BRINNON PIONEER--LILLIAN CHRISTIANSEN

When Mother, Sarah Miller, a young widow with three children living at Symes, Colorado, received letters from her sister in Brinnon, Washington, telling of the great trees many feet to the first limb, of the river teaming with salmon, of the thousands of wild ducks on the Bay, of a potato that made a dinner for five, of a cabbage head that weighed pounds--that sounded to Mother like The Promised Land.

She began packing up to go out West. She baked loaves of bread, churned plenty of butter, picked wild red raspberries, made jam, sold her cows, and boarded the train for Denver. There we took a tourist train for Seattle, Washington. The journey was pleasant, we youngsters quiet and well behaved--Mother saw to that.

We arrived in Seattle the latter part of September, 1892. Stayed at the Alaska House until the little steamer "Delta" was ready to make her weekly trip along Hood Canal. Captain Libby was master of the "Delta".

In late afternoon, we arrived at Brinnon. There was no dock. A man rowed out to meet the boat and, as he drew along side, he heard Mother getting us youngsters ready to land. He, a Kentuckian, sang out to her, "Hello thar, Missouri!" Her speech betrayed her--my tall, resolute Mother with beautiful rich auburn hair and the face of a German Madonna.

We were handed down into the boat. When we were all seated there was little of the rim above water. We had never been in a row boat. The deep water around us, the dark green woods clear to the edge of high tide, the strangeness of it all was rather frightening but we were soon setting our feet on the Promised Land. Our destination, a little logging camp, at what is now the Coates Place (between Swansons and Seal Rock Camp).

Nothing exciting happened as we went stumbling over the slippery stones of the beach until we came upon a great fish. To my brother who had seen nothing larger than suckers and chubs from the South Platte, this was unbelievable. He took the monster by the tail and we started on. It was heavy for an eleven year old boy so he laid it in a safe place and decided to come back after it.

We resumed our walk and were met with a warm, hearty welcome. Tom did not return for the dead dog salmon.

Our aunt was cook at the camp. Bob, our nineteen year old cousin, took care of the four yoke of oxen used to haul the logs over the skid road to the salt water where they were made up into booms for the tug boat to tow to the sawmill.

The skids were greased for smoother running. That was a job an eleven year old boy could do. So, with a big can of vile-smelling oil in one hand, a gunnysack swab on the end of a stick in the other hand. My brother Tom dipped the swab in the oil and gave each skid a slap or two. The oil was made from decomposed dogfish livers.

One of Bob's jobs was to shoe the oxen. A frame of logs stood near the ox hovel. Into this frame, called the Stocks, or Slings, Bob would lead Brigham, McGintey, Star, or whichever ox needed shoeing, time him good, put a wide band of woven hay rope under him, fasten the ends to poles that could be turned with wooden pegs in augur holes. He would hoist the ox up so he could tie the foot in position to nail the shoe on. Rarely the ox took quietly to being shod. It was hard work. Bob also drove the ox team.

A neighbor drove on the Duckabush was an expert ox teamster. He walked along beside his team, ox goad across his forearm, telling them short and sharp to "Whoa Ho!" or "Gee Buck!", plying the goad like a riddle bow. He knew and loved oxen like some men know and love fine horses.

There was a family on every one hundred and sixty acres of land along the Dosewallips River. The last family lived above what is now the Archer place. The men who worked in the camp put in twelve hours a day. Those whose homes were too far away to go home every night slept in the bunk house. Every Saturday night they filled their pack sacks with groceries and started homeward with from sixty to ninety pound packs on their backs, walking six or seven miles.

The largest families used a fifty-pound sack of flour a week. There were few luxuries in those pack sacks. Those men, too, had come to the Promised Land.

The townsite of Arbaculla had been laid out at Pleasant Harbor and the townsite of Jupiter City at, or near, what is now Seal Rock. Everything was in readiness and waiting for the sure coming of the railroad along the Olympic Peninsula.

Among the men were carpenters, a millwright, a painter and paper hanger, brewer and brick maker. The Yelwick place used to be called the Brickyard.

There was a real depression in those days. Quoting from the Readers Digest of October, 1857, "The nation was then in the grip of the worst depression and money panic it had ever known."

A young German captain came inquiring for Jupiter City. Answers were vague. He impatiently exclaimed, "We know more about Jupiter City in San Francisco than you do here!" It was said that he was seen clinging to a cow's tail through Brinnon in snow four feet deep. His stay was short.

The winter of '93-'94 the snow laid four feet deep to the water's edge.

For amusement, dances were held in homes where there was room enough. The little school house near the camp was too small. Later they built a log school house at the foot of Brinnon Hill where the school now stands. The fiddlers took turns playing what tunes they knew. The caller sang out, "Choose your partners for a quadrille". And with "Salute your partners", the dance was on. They quadrilled, waltzed and two-stepped into the wee hours.

They had picnics and clam bakes. An old sea captain made the clam chowder like they made it in the state of Maine. He had been captain of a whaling vessel before the ports of Japan were open to foreign ships. He used to visit the school sometimes and tell interesting things.

Two ministers came to Brinnon and a little Sunday School was started in the school house. Christmas Eve, 1892, we gathered there, sang and spoke Christmas pieces, and a little Christmas tree stood bravely in one corner with some candles and simple trimming.

Before going to bed that night I trustingly hung up my stocking. Christmas morn there it hung--in the toe a pretzel. Neighbor children had come by while I was asleep and shared their Christmas with me--a sad Christmas for those five children--their mother had taken her life.

At last came spring and a warm Chinook wind helped melt the snow that had laid on so long and frozen so hard we walked on top of it.

The next outstanding event for us youngsters was when school started. There were about twelve pupils enrolled. They walked to school carrying their lunches in five-pound lard pails.

In August, 1893, Mother married Mr. Wolcott, a widower who had a homestead and nothing. Mother had three children and nothing.

We walked the trail four and a half miles deeper into the Promised Land, packing and carrying to the little two-room log house chinked with moss. The roof was of shakes. The floors were puncheon smoothed down with the adz. The windows were small--a corner cupboard held the few ironstone china dishes and what groceries we had. One of the things I learned was to fold and cut newspaper into fancy-edged shelf paper. Mother later papered the walls with the Seattle P.I. which came weekly.

The largest room served as bedroom, dining room and kitchen. Our cooking utensils were three iron pots, two bread pans, a tin kettle with holes in the bottom to set over a kettle of boiling water to steam contents, frying pan & an iron tea kettle we named Dinah.

Our diet at first was white bread, beans, potatoes and gravy made with lard, flour and water. That summer there were wild blackberries.

The other room was bedroom and sitting room. In one end of this room Dad had built a clay fireplace. He built the chimney of sticks plastered inside and out with clay. It lasted for several years until it caught fire.

Our table was homemade with an oilcloth cover. Our bedsteads were homemade. For mattresses Mother made ticks and filled them with pea straw. Dad had broadcast some field peas and thrashed them out with a flail made of two round sticks, the ends tied loosely together with a buckskin thong. On top of the straw ticks Mother put cotton ticks with cotton pads covered with flour sacks and tied like a quilt.

Our home remedies were a bottle of arnica and a little box of quinine. The quinine was taken straight from the point of the big blade in Dad's jackknife, followed with a drink of cold water. We learned of cascara. We called it bearberry. Dad would cut some strips of bark and make tea of it--so bitter.

Our clothing was rather dark in color and of material that would "wear well". Dutch blue calico wore well. Flour sacks were prized for pillow cases, underwear and any uses they could be put to. Shoes were coarse button shoes for Mother and me--a pair a year. Men wore logger shoes and drove hobnails or calks in them--hard on floors but a necessity in the woods.

In every home was a lantern to carry after dark. A neighbor along the trail often stopped at a homestead and borrowed the lantern when darkness overtook them.

In every home there was a rifle. Dad's was a 45-90. He had a set of reloading tools. He melted lead in a small crucible, poured it into the mould, the bullet came out so hot and shining like pure silver. He pressed a cap into the ned of the empty shell. There was a tiny brass dipper for measuring the gun powder. He poured a dipper of powder in the empty shell and with a little hand clamp pressed the bullet in place, and when he had several cartridges loaded, Dad went hunting.

That was hard country to hunt in--no one hunted for sport. Sometimes out all night, he came home tired, wet and gray-faced and not always with venison. When news came to our valley that a hunter over on the Duck-a-bush had come upon a band of elk and shot them all, some homesteaders went over there, hoping to save the meat. It was too late. If they had gotten their hands on that hunter he would have been punished.

Our first winter on the homestead Dad worked in the camp. The youngest, Carl, four years old, became so sick. A young doctor from Port Townsend happened to be in Brinnon. He came. It was brain fever. Carl died on April 7, 1894. The Olympic Mountains around us, and what sky we could see grey and dripping--it seemed like the sun had forgotten how to shine and Mother had forgotten how to smile.

Dad walked to Leland, some 18 or 20 miles away and bought a cow which he led home. She, too, became a pioneer. There was no pasture, pitiful small stack of hay and such a tiny clearing on which to raise anything. She had to forage in the woods, sometimes across the river.

Every homestead had a cross-cut saw. The boys sawed wood. It took a lot of it and they helped their fathers clear land. Girls were taught to bake bread and sew a straight seam. They washed dishes, carrying water from the brooks. They were mother's helpers.

We all feared cougars and there were grounds for our fears. I had seen the head and hide of one that had killed a cow on a homestead above us. And there were many stories of cougars trying to carry off babies and small children.

One day a big cloud of smoke over on the Duckabush was getting bigger and blacker. When the flames began leaping along the crest of the mountain, we became frightened. However, when the fire began burning down the north side of the mountain it lost its fury. We watched it into the night until we felt secure to go to bed.

We must have a school. Dad donated land. A neighbor, father of seven children, walked to Port Townsend, some forty-five miles, and went before the County Commissioners, pleading for a school. There was opposition but finally his plea was granted and a log school house built. Dad made double seats. The desks were of a single split cedar board. He went to the woods for his materials. He made the blackboards and erasers. Soon came the first day of school in the new school house. Our first teacher, a young lady from Port Townsend.

At one time thirty-two pupils were enrolled in the Upriver school. All grades taught from first to tenth. The teacher heard forty classes a day. Her pay-forty five dollars a month. One year we had an eight months term. Usually we had six or seven.

The Mount Constance Congregational Church was organized. We had no resident pastor and no regular church services. Sometimes Rev. Young used to come across Hood Canal, walk upriver and hold services in the Upriver school house. Later, Rev. Eels rowed his boat from Tahouya to Brinnon. He, too, walked upriver and held meetings. They came, rain or shine, the light of consecration in their faces.

A neighbor became Superintendent of our Sunday School and it was rated among, if not the best, in the State. Parents came with their children to church, Sunday School and prayer meetings. At Christmas time the school house was decorated with festoons of Elkhorn moss and ferns, a tree stood in one corner with candles and trimming. The place was filled. The recitations and songs lasted until near midnight when Santa Claus arrived to distribute the bags of hard candy and nuts. No one was left out.

Times began to be better--labor, market, everything took on new life. With saw, axe, mattock, shovel and grub hoe, calloused hands, sweat and tired back, Dad was enlarging the clearing. Finally he acquired a team and the clearing went faster with its help. Mother kept chickens and traded eggs for groceries and feed. The trail widened to accommodate cart and wagon. The days of pack sack and pack saddle were over.

In the winter with the rain coming down on the shake roof, we, snug and warm in our beds, wakened to Mother getting breakfast by lamp light, fire in the kitchen stove crackling, "Dinah" bubbling away and Mother grinding coffee. Our lives in the little log home in the Olympics had taken on meaning and purpose and security. But there were responsibilities not always pleasant--Tom learned to pull teeth with homemade forceps and one time a boy got a fish hook caught in his nose and Tom had to file the hook in two to get it out.

Sorrow came to neighbor's family when one of their small boys fell from a foot log and drowned. The wonderful kindness of neighbors in time of trouble!

Some of the upriver folks joined a Lodge which held meetings in Brinnon. Three Upriver boys went off to the Spanish-American War.

Our amusement was play parties. held in the homes. We pulled taffy, played games, sang and danced Weavelly Wheat, Brass Wagon, Tide-O into the wee hours. On the Fourth of July, boys would fire their fathers' rifle a few times. We met at the school house, sang patriotic songs, some spoke patriotic pieces and always the Declaration of Independence was read.

The summer of 1899 the school house was decorated for a wedding, seats were filled and folks standing. The bride, eldest of eight, living across the river, came walking down the steep slanting foot log, dressed in white cross-bar muslin, tan shoes and a white hat with plumes. Little sisters of bride and groom scattered rose petals along the aisle. The teacher struck up the Wedding March on the new organ. The bride marched slowly in on the arm of her father to where the groom, best men and bridesmaids were waiting. Rev. Eels performed the ceremony and the newlyweds, amid kisses and congratulations, stepped into the spring wagon and drove away, leaving the scent of roses and us girls to sigh and dream. Afterward the bride's father was heard to say "That weddin' cost me $20!"

Mother loved to garden. Dad fenced in a fine garden spot with picket fence. She had rows of flowers, strawberries and vegetables. Dad kept clearing land. There was need for hay and pasture as our livestock, increased.

When a large area was thrown into the Olympic Forest Reserve the line fell not far above us. The homesteaders in the Reserve started moving out. Mother had always feared the river--she had seen much of the cleared land on the adjoining homestead melt away into that river. A logging company came in and began buying up the timber to log with locomotive. The days of ox teams were gone. Mother and Dad sold their timber. Our little log home with two rooms added, a good new barn, good out-buildings, some fruit trees coming into bearing, twenty-two acres of land cleared and fenced, and hay and pasture for the team and seven cows sold to a neighbor for six hundred dollars. Our homestead is now the Donahue place.

It was a good life--it was a hard life.

I have dipped my pen in the past and bring my memories to a close with this lovely verse by Grace Crowell.

I have found such joy in simple things-- A plain,
clean room, a nut brown loaf of bread,
A cup of milk, a kettle as it sings,
The shelter of a roof above my head,
And in a leaf-faced square upon a floor,
There yellow sunlight glimmers through a door.

I have found such joy in things that fill
My quiet days: a curtain's blowing grace,
A growing plant upon a window sill,
A rose, fresh-cut and placed within a vase;
A table cleared, a lamp beside a chair,
And books I long have loved beside me there.

Oh, I have found such joy I wish I might
Tell every woman who goes seeking far
For some elusive, feverish delight,
That very close to home the great joys are;
These fundamental things--old as the race
Yet never, through the ages, common place.

Elkhorn moss and ferns

MEMORIES OF A HOOD CANAL BOAT CAPTAIN--
CAPTAIN TORGER BIRKLAND

Seventy years ago last June, at the age of ten, I arrived here from Norway with my parents and five brothers and sisters and settled in the deep forest near the shores of Hood Canal.

Our family learned to love this rugged country and became a living part of it very soon. Our living came from the woods. It was hard work, ten-hour working days, six days a week in logging camps which were plentiful in those days.

And now, today, as we smoothly glide over the same waters and view the familiar landscape, many fond memories return.

I have been privileged to live through one of the most exciting and interesting periods of time in recorded history. I feel it so unfair that our children's children should be denied the pleasure of having even a small parcel of these hundreds of acres of forest lands with adjoining miles of the most beautiful beaches in the world to call their own.

I suppose this new thing planned (Trident), in addition to what is already at Bangor, is by some called progress, but by those of us who remember it as it was, it's tragic that so many people should be deprived of this ideal vacation and residential land on this most beautiful part of Hood Canal.

Where the docks are now located was a little logging camp with buildings on log rafts on the beach, afloat on high water and at low tide on a slant on the beach.

It was at this camp at the age of eleven, well, nearly twelve, I had my first job as "whistle punk." There, in just a few months, it seemed, I grew to manhood and became a full-fledged lumberjack. It would be interesting to go into this a little deeper but inasmuch as I am supposed to talk about boats on Hood Canal, we'll have to get into this more at a later date.

Logging camps must have food and other supplies, and the only means of transportation on Hood Canal was by boat, so then instead of building docks, every camp had a raft anchored out in deep water where the steamer would land.

The *Perdita* was the first passenger and freight boat that I saw on this body of water. She came into our camp about twice a week with canned goods and fresh meat. This was usually at the noon hour so we all had a good look at the boat. It really added something to the day and was looked forward to by all hands.

Camps where horses were used for hauling logs (which was the most common at that time) received the bulk of the ship's cargo, such as baled hay and oats for feed and large wooden stave barrels of crude oil used for greasing the skids. These barrels were usually rolled out through the port and overboard to be picked up by the boom man and towed to the beach by him.

Grease barrels would always float but one time one went to the bottom. A few days later a call came out from the Seattle dock office for a barrel of molasses that had somehow got mixed in with the grease barrels. The molasses barrel was never found.

About 1905 the steamer *Inland Flyer* came on the run for a short time. This boat had just then been converted from coal to oil and was the first in the "Mosquito Fleet" to burn oil.

Prior to the 1900s nearly all of the steamers used wood for fuel and had regular cordwood refueling stations along the route.

In 1906, I believe, the *Lydia Thompson* came on the run for about a year. Next came the sternwheel steamer *State of Washington.*

This romantic old boat served the canal well for five or six years at which time the Puget Sound Navigation Company came out with the spanking new steel steamer *Potlatch* built at the Moran yards in Seattle in 1912, especially for the prosperous Hood Canal run.

It was my privilege in 1916 to ship on the *Potlatch* as deckhand, and in 1917 as second mate. This was a great little ship. At 9:00 a.m. we took our departure from Seattle, stopped at Maxwelton and Austin on Whidbey Island. From there across Admiralty Inlet to Port Ludlow, then to Port Gamble, then Lofall and Bangor about noon and also some logging camp stops in between.

From Bangor to Hazel Point and Coyle, then to Seabeck and then across to Brinnon. From Brinnon to

Duckabush where the old fellow came out to meet us with his big rowboat.

From there to Triton's Cove and across to Nellita along the shore to Holly and to the peninsula side again to Eldon and the Hamma Hamma. Perhaps I should relate an incident here.

Offshore from Crawford and Nelson's logging camp, we stopped to discharge camp supplies into a large skiff. Boxes of canned goods, sacks of flour and sugar and a quarter of beef were piled in. Space was left in the bottom for a bunch of boom chains. The skiff was already low in the water and it was suggested to the young man, Mr. Crawford's son, in the boat that "these heavy chains will overload the boat." But he insisted and the chains were gently dropped in. The cargo was all there and lastly Mr. Crawford, the father, who had been to town also got into the overloaded boat. We let go, shoved them off and wished them luck. When about ten feet away, water was seen rushing in over the gunwales and the boat went down like a rock.

Captain Carl Stevens of the *Potlatch*, who was standing on the bridge taking in this whole performance, immediately sounded the boat alarm and in about three minutes a lifeboat was in the water. Mr. Crawford, who was floating with an oar under each arm, was picked up first. The young fellow had struck out for shore. Everything that was afloat, including sacks of flour, was picked up and taken to the beach. This was all considered part of a day's work on Hood Canal. Horses for logging camps were, like the skid grease, backed up to the port and shoved overboard to swim ashore.

We still had some landings--Dewato, Lilliwaup, Hoodsport, and Potlatch. Before arrival at Union City, the end of the long run, arriving there around 6:30 p.m., departing Union 7:00 for the return trip, making numerous stops to take on loggers and during vacation season, people were on the move with camping gear and fishing outfits.

There were as yet no roads, therefore, no automobiles to rush around in. Everyone appeared so relaxed and good natured. The arrival time in Seattle was around 4:00 a.m., but the passengers were allowed to occupy the staterooms until six o'clock.

As I look back, there was never a dull moment in this steamboat life. One morning about one minute before leaving time, an express man came tearing into the dock, his long-legged horse at full trot right up to the slip, then came to a sudden halt. A middle-aged man jumped out of the seat where he'd been riding with the teamster, ran to the back of the wagon, grabbed a hold of the leather strap on the end of a large trunk, yanked it off with a bang, dragged it a few feet to the edge of the slip and started down. The tide was way down low and the slip was steep. The man was in such a rush that he hadn't noticed that the cargo plank was in and the steamer was ready to sail.

Everything went well until he got about two-thirds down where the slip was quite often submerged and slippery when he lost control. He and the trunk went headlong into the bay.

Mr. Frank E. Burns, the company's general manager, on his way to the office, out on the end of the dock, stopped by to see how things were going on the *Potlatch* just in time for the final act.

When Mr. Burns saw the men on the boat cast ring buoys and other ropes in the water, he quickly noticed the trunk was drifting off and sung out to the boat crew, "Get the trunk, never mind the man, get the trunk."

You see, the man had by then grabbed a hold of a cross brace on a pile and was thought to be safe. The port captain, who was also looking on, informed Mr. Burns, "that's not our baggage check on there, Mr. Burns," and Mr. Burns again sang out, "Get the man then, never mind the trunk." The man and the trunk were both rescued.

Sundays, during the summer months, was a great day for us all on this run. We ran a capacity load excursion direct from Colman dock to Union City. The steamer *City of Angeles* was also put in service here during July and August to carry a capacity overflow load of excursionists.

At times I have a longing for those wonderful days on Hood Canal with the old steamboats to live again.

In late fall, 1917, the services of this fine little ship, the *Potlatch*, came to an end on Hood Canal.

Roads had been completed pretty well around from Shelton and also a narrow road to Bremerton. So here the automobile commenced to dig in and take its toll.

We now transferred to the smaller and more economical operating *City of Angeles* for the balance of the winter. Soon she, too, was taken off and the freighter *Aloha* then became the last vessel to serve Hood Canal.

Now, a few words about the beginning of boat service on this enchanting body of water, on this I stand to be corrected.

Captain Daniel Troutman owned the steamer *Delta*, sixty nine feet long and built in 1889, and was to my knowledge the first passenger vessel in regular service to Seattle for several years. When she became too small, Troutman replaced her with the steamer *Dode* (a vessel that I, too, remember).

An oldtime shipmate of mine, Captain C. T. Wyatt, received his first job as deckhand on the *Delta*; Cyp., as he was affectionately called, came to Holly on the canal when a child and grew up there.

Edwin E. Eells, son of the missionary and Indian agent of the Twanoh tribe on the reservation at Union, was chief mate on the *Potlatch* when I was there.

All those oldtimers have long since crossed the bar but fond memories remain.

Potlatch (Puget Sound Maritime Historical Society)

MEMORIES OF A SEABECK PIONEER--ALICE GERTRUDE NICKELS WALTON

We came from Pitchden, Maine and when we landed, there were several Indians on the wharf, but no white men. I asked mother if they were the only kind of people who lived there. I had never seen Indians before. I thought they looked horrible and I was afraid of them.

The sawmill employed many skilled workmen. Our vessel was reloaded with lumber for San Francisco. At the end of the dock there were a general merchandise store and a two-story building. The first floor was a cookhouse and diningroom for the men and the second floor was a community hall. We had Sunday school every Sunday afternoon and church services once a month and a dance every Saturday.

There was a small red schoolhouse, also a hotel which was later named the Eagle Hotel and several saloons and a Chinese Laundry. Transportation was poor. There were no roads, only Indian trails. We had to depend on sailing vessels. The *Kate Alexander*, a one-masted sloop, brought mail from Port Gamble once a week, usually but not always, because we could not always depend on the wind. Later a small steamer, the *St. Patrick*, brought mail two or three times a week and carried passengers.

Fresh meat was scarce. The company bought a lot of hogs and turned them out in the town. There were troughs back of the cookhouse where the hogs used to be fed a barrel of refuse a meal. Every Saturday, there was a fresh dressed hog hanging at the cookhouse and any of the families could buy pork there.

A new schoolhouse was built next to the old one in 1877. It was fixed up in first class shape, plastered, with fine new blackboards, a new library and a second hand piano. We were very proud of our school. There were seventy pupils and one teacher; the older pupils helped the younger ones with their lessons. Our books were bought by our parents. Some were poor and had no books and had to borrow from those who had.

In 1880, six feet of snow fell in one night. The roof of the school was too flat and not supported in the middle and it collapsed, destroying everything. It was a great disappointment. The little red schoolhouse was used until the present one was built.

After the roof caved in, the teacher used to take us all into the grove back of the school to hear our lessons, rather than keep us shut in the stuffy little one-room of the old schoolhouse. There was a beautiful grove there, where we used to have Sunday school picnics.

A barkentine christened *Olympus* was the first sailing vessel ever built on Puget Sound; the *Cassandra Adams,* named for Mr. Adams' wife, was built at Seabeck. Then some smaller ones were built for Mexico. One was named the *American Boy.*

I was fifteen years of age then and Mr. H. Doncaster, the building commander of the *American Boy,* asked me to christen the boat, as he said I reminded him of his daughter who was dead. This was a great honor and necessitated a new dress. Mother made me a white swiss with a great many ruffles.

When the important day arrived, I didn't want anyone to see my dress until the last moment, so I put on a cape and went to the launching grounds and was taken up the plank to the bow. Then my cape was slipped off and Mr. Doncaster gave me a bottle of champagne tied with red, white and blue ribbons. At the right time, a signal was given and with the help of a man who held my arm, I broke the bottle and the *American Boy* slid into the Canal. There were no people on board.

The ship rested on its keel with planks on each side to support it upright. When it was ready to be launched, the men knocked the scaffolds away and the ship began to move down to the water and into the water, and gathered speed and went almost to the other side before it stopped. When you heard the men knocking the planks away, it sounded dangerous, but no one was ever hurt at a launching.

Two other steamers were built and launched, a sternwheeler named *Louise* and a tug named *Richard Holyoke* in honor of the manager of the mill.

Sailing vessels from many ports, South America, Australia, and other countries, came to Seabeck for lumber. These sailing vessels had to be towed in from Cape Flattery. As a vessel rounded Hazel Point, the whistle at the mill blew one long blast and we all knew a ship was coming.

Crews on the vessels talked strange languages. Some looked like Indians but were very tall. We were used to our Indians who were different. Our Indians lived in shacks built of odd pieces of lumber down on the beach. Some of the Indian children went to our school. But I was always a little afraid of the grown ones and when they came near our house for water or wood, I stayed indoors.

A weekly dance was held with an organ and a violin for music. We had square dances and the waltz. Sometimes supper was served in the cook house on the first floor. Christmas trees where everyone received presents was part of the community fun. There were two large trees one Christmas. The Sunday school gave entertainment and also the little red schoolhouse pupils.

In the fall of 1886, a vessel was unloading freight with a donkey engine and a spark from the engine ignited a lumber pile. A heavy south wind was blowing and swept the flames to the two mills and the shops. The men worked hard all day but by night nothing but ruins was left. The heat was so great that it cooked the apples on the trees in the orchard near the road. It was a terrible day but none of the men were hurt. The fire left many out of work and most of the families moved away.

I was always a kind of scardy cat. I hadn't been married very long and wasn't use to keeping house and being alone all day. We lived on the other side of town, away from everybody and I always stayed in the house with the door locked. The day of the fire, I didn't know anything had happened and I saw a crowd of women in the road, coming toward my house. Well, I thought, what kind of women are they, flinging their arms around like that? They came and knocked on the door, but I hid. But they called and told me what had happened, so I unlocked the door. Lots of the women knelt right down in the road and prayed, that day.

Seabeck was deserted. The town lay dormant for many years. Some houses were sold and moved away, others were torn down and the rest crumbled. The late Lawrence Colman bought the town site and saved

Seabeck. The cookhouse was moved across the pond and became the present chapel. Houses and the hotel were repaired, so the original quaintness was kept and the whole tract became a beautiful conference grounds. During the summer, many religious organizations meet here. Thanks are due to Mr. Colman for his contribution to Seabeck in preserving the mill site and making it an ideal spot for rest and inspiration.

I remember Mr. Clayson. One reason I know for his dislike of the mill company was that he had a saloon and hotel. To get to it the men had to cross a wooden bridge. There were two other saloons in town and the men used to make the rounds of them. There were always intoxicated men in the town, lying around in the ditches, but we didn't think anything of it. They always kept their place. But Mr. Holyoke didn't like the men to drink so much that they couldn't work. So he had the bridge cut to keep them from going to Mr. Clayson's place.

Seabeck

THE WILLIAM H. SCHWEIZER
DOCUMENTARY LIBRARY
from
EOS PUBLISHING

The William H. Schweizer Documentary Library stands for the finest in adult and young adult nonfiction. Every title meets the most rigorous standards of research, photography, art, and literary excellence. Readers will enjoy these timeless, positive, entertaining, educational, and inspirational books. The following books are offered by the William H. Schweizer Documentary Library:

Beyond Understanding: The complete guide to... Princess Louisa, Chatterbox Falls, Jervis Inlet

Solemn Silence: The complete guide to... Hood Canal by Land and Sea

Born Free: The complete guide to... the Mighty Columbia River by Land and River (publication date 1994)

These titles are available at your favorite bookstore or directly from the publisher. The William H. Schweizer Documentary Library also offers Ansel Adams quality prints and wildlife prints. To order any of these books, or for a current catalog and price schedule, including quality copyrighted prints, write to:

William H. Schweizer Documentary Library
EOS Publishing
331 Andover Park East
Seattle, Washington 98188
206-575-1919